BLUE COFFEE

Books available by Adrian Mitchell

POETRY

For Beauty Douglas: Collected Poems 1953-79 (Allison & Busby, 1982)
Love Songs of World War Three (Allison & Busby/W.H. Allen, 1989)
Greatest Hits: His 40 Golden Greats (Bloodaxe Books, 1991)
Blue Coffee: Poems 1985-1996 (Bloodaxe Books, 1996)
Heart on the Left: Poems 1953-1984 (Bloodaxe Books, 1997)

PLAYS

The Pied Piper (Oberon Books)
Gogol: The Government Inspector (Methuen)
Calderón: The Mayor of Zalamea & two other plays (Absolute Classics)
Lope de Vega: Fuente Ovejuna and Lost in a Mirror (Absolute Classics)
Tyger Two, Man Friday, Satie Day/Night and *In the Unlikely Event of an Emergency* (Oberon Books)

POETRY FOR CHILDREN

The Orchard Book of Poems (Orchard, 1993)
The Thirteen Secrets of Poetry (Macdonald, 1993)

CHILDREN'S STORIES

Our Mammoth
Our Mammoth Goes to School
Our Mammoth in the Snow
The Baron Rides Out
The Baron on the Island of Cheese
The Baron All at Sea
    (all Walker Books)

The Ugly Duckling (Dorling Kindersley)
Maudie and the Green Children (Tradewind)
Gynormous! The Ultimate Book of Giants (Orion)

BLUE COFFEE

POEMS 1985-1996

Adrian Mitchell

BLOODAXE BOOKS

ISBN: 1 85224 362 7

First published 1996 by
Bloodaxe Books Ltd,
P.O. Box 1SN,
Newcastle upon Tyne NE99 1SN.

Bloodaxe Books Ltd acknowledges
the financial assistance of Northern Arts.

Cover printing by J. Thomson Colour Printers Ltd, Glasgow.

Printed in Great Britain by
Bell & Bain Limited, Glasgow, Scotland.

This book is in memory of Boty Goodwin,
artist and writer, and of her parents
Pauline Boty and Clive Goodwin

ACKNOWLEDGEMENTS

Most of the poems in this book have been performed before being printed. They have been printed in the *Guardian, New Statesman & Society, Stand, Ambit, Scratch, Casablanca, London Review of Books, Tribune, London Magazine, Poetry Review* and other magazines, and also broadcast on TV's *Words on Film, Newsnight* and *The Late Show.*

Thanks are especially due to Nanyang University in Singapore for their Fellowship in Drama, to Cambridge University for making me the Judith E. Wilson Fellow, and Swansea UK Year of Literature for the special honour of being the first Dylan Thomas Fellow in 1995. All these people helped me make this book.

EDUCATIONAL HEALTH WARNING

None of the work in this or any other of my books is to be used in connection with any examination whatsoever. Reduce the size of classes in State schools to twelve and I might reconsider.

CONTENTS

COUNTRY LIFE

SOME ANIMALS

JOIN THE POETRY AND SEE THE WORLD

YOUNG AND OLD

BOTY

YES

A Puppy Called Puberty

It was like keeping a puppy in your underpants
A secret puppy you weren't allowed to show to anyone
Not even your best friend or your worst enemy

You wanted to pat him stroke him cuddle him
All the time but you weren't supposed to touch him

He only slept for five minutes at a time
Then he'd suddenly perk up his head
In the middle of school medical inspection
And always on bus rides
So you had to climb down from the upper deck
All bent double to smuggle the puppy off the bus
Without the buxom conductress spotting
Your wicked and ticketless stowaway.

Jumping up, wet-nosed, eagerly wagging –
He only stopped being a nuisance
When you were alone together
Pretending to be doing your homework
But really gazing at each other
Through hot and hazy daydreams

Of those beautiful schoolgirls on the bus
With kittens bouncing in their sweaters.

A Dog Called Elderly

And now I have a dog called Elderly
And all he ever wants to do
Is now and then be let out for a piss
But spend the rest of his lifetime
Sleeping on my lap in front of the fire.

Questionnaire

Q. How do you do?
A. Like a bear in the Zoo.
Q. Why should that be?
A. The world is not free.
Q. Must it always be so?
A. No.
   With our hearts and our brains
   We will tear off its chains.
Q. You write poems, why?
A. Because I am shy.
   In real life I conceal
   Everything that I feel,
   But in poems I shout
   And my feelings fly out.
Q. Why do you write in verse at all?
A. I would always rather jump than crawl,
   My tongue would rather sing than talk
   And my feet would sooner dance than walk.
Q. What's the difference between a walker and dancer?
A. Love is the answer.
Q. Why do you write?
A.   For the love of life
   And my friends, my animals,
   my children and my wife.
   I am lucky and happy –
Q. But how do you do?
A. Like a bear who dreams he is not in a Zoo.

Yes

A smile says: Yes.
A heart says: Blood.
When the rain says: Drink
The earth says: Mud.

The kangaroo says: Trampoline.
Giraffes say: Tree.
A bus says: Us
While a car says: Me.

Lemon trees say: Lemons.
A jug says: Lemonade.
The villain says: You're wonderful.
The hero: I'm afraid.

The forest says: Hide and Seek.
The grass says: Green and Grow.
The railway says: Maybe.
The prison says: No.

The millionaire says: Take.
The beggar says: Give.
The soldier cries: Mother!
The baby sings: Live.

The river says: Come with me.
The moon says: Bless.
The stars says: Enjoy the light.
The sun says: Yes.

Golo, the Gloomy Goalkeeper

Golo plays for the greatest soccer team in the Universe.
They are so mighty that their opponents never venture out of
        their own penalty area.
They are so all–conquering that Golo never touches the ball during
        a match, and very seldom sees it.
Every game seems to last a lifetime to Golo, the Gloomy Goalkeeper.

Golo scratches white paint off the goalposts' surface to reveal the
 silver shining underneath.
He kisses the silver of the goalpost.
It does not respond.

Golo counts the small stones in the penalty area.
There are three hundred and seventy eight, which is not his lucky
 number.
Golo pretends to have the hiccups, then says to himself, imitating
 his sister's voice:
Don't breathe, and just die basically.

Golo breaks eight small sticks in half.
Then he has sixteen very small sticks.
He plants geranium seeds along the goal-line.
He paints a picture of a banana and sells it to the referee at half-time.

Golo finds, among the bootmarks in the dust, the print of one
 stiletto heel.
He crawls around on all fours doing lion imitations.
He tries to read his future in the palm of his hand, but forgets to
 take his glove off.
He writes a great poem about butterflies but tears it up because
 he can't think of a rhyme for Wednesday.
He knits a sweater for the camel in the Zoo.

Golo suddenly realises he can't remember if he is a man or a woman.
He takes a quick look, but still can't decide.
Golo makes up his mind that grass is his favourite colour.
He puts on boots, track-suit, gloves and hat all the same colour as
 grass.
He paints his face a gentle shade of green.

Golo lies down on the pitch and becomes invisible.
The grass tickles the back of his neck.
At last Golo is happy.
He has fallen in love with the grass.
And the grass has fallen in love with Golo, the Gloomy Goalkeeper.

Blood and Oil
(to the British armed forces)

And once again the politicians
Whose greatest talent is for lying
Are sending you where they're afraid to go
To do their killing and dying

You're young and you've been trained to fight
You're brave, well-equipped and loyal.
That's why they're sending you to Hell –
    Blood and Oil.

It's not to defend the Falklands sheep
Or Christians in Ireland
But to sit in a tank till you are moved
On a giant chessboard of desert sand

You're not there to fight against tyranny
Or for hostages or British soil
But for economics, the dollars of death –
    Blood and Oil.

And the soldiers you fight will be young men
With no reason to kill, young men like you
With beautiful families back home
And some with wives and children too

But no politicians will be there
When lungs tear and arteries boil
They'll be filmed with survivors in hospital
    Blood and Oil.

Yes, once again the politicians
Whose greatest talent is for lying
Are sending young men where old men dare not go
To do their killing and dying
To do their killing and dying
To do their killing and dying

Blood and Oil
Blood and Oil
Blood and Oil

Blood and oil...

No, She Really is Upset, You Know

I hate these sensible conversations
Where you pick up a problem – Lucy is very upset
because of what Wendy said about Bill –
And you examine the Lucy problem like a pretty tea-cup
And you comment on it, saying perhaps we should really
call it a Wendy problem or maybe a Bill problem
And you pass it on and everyone takes a turn
Looking at the problem and commenting and passing it on
I would rather go out and throw problems at a wall
or be in a jungle conversation of overflow and overlap
Or jump from non sequitur to non sequitur across the swamp
And to hell with Lucy and to hell with Wendy and Bill
To be upset is to be a pretty tea-cup
And pretty tea-cups are always getting upset
Well my advice is boil up a kettle and make another cup of tea
Or better still go out and buy a bottle of something you
never drank before and share it with a friend or a
stranger in a bus shelter or a desert
Upset?
That's what Claudius said to Hamlet:
Can't you see you're making your mother very upset?
If he hadn't asked that Fortinbras wouldn't have marched into
        Elsinore
To find the whole castle knee-deep in terrible dank tea-leaves
And turn around to the audience and say:
Go, bid the soldiers make a nice cuppa.

Millennium Countdown

Nine will coo you with a beeper bomb
Eight will tickle the mousetrap
Seven will shave you like a zombie prom
Six is the ultimate cowpat
Five will catch you in a yellow thumb zone
Four will play the Hempty Dempty
Three will be lost in abalone Babylone
Two will find your pooter empty
Some say One will be miserable fun
Some say Bake the town down
But I say if you count me count me out
Millennium Countdown

Bruce Thursday
Minority shine
Sliding all over the meltdown
You bit it – you git it –
Harna! Harna!
Millennium Countdown

Can't stop dreaming about the future
Two thousand years in a beggar's coat
Can't stop screaming about the factoid future
Two thousand years got stuck in my throat

Trying Hard To Be Normal
(for Spike Milligan)

I bought myself a hairbrush
A Military Hairbrush it turned out
It came in a box marked Military Hairbrush
I opened the box
And took out the Military Hairbrush
But there was still something left in the box
I shook the box and brought out a brochure
It was printed in every colour that exists
The brochure showed me with diagrams
And a text in seven languages
How to brush my hair with the Military Hairbrush
I was about to throw the box away
When I realised there was something else left in the box
I shook the box and out dropped
A smaller brush
A wooden brush a humble brush
Certainly not a military brush
Just a brush
I looked for an explanation in the brochure
And found that this was the brush
With which to brush
The Military Hairbrush

Or

Simplicity
is a glass of water
Stupidity
is a mugful of dust
Simplicity
is the moonlight's daughter
Stupidity
is the father of rust

get the idea
they are opposites
they are not twins
get the idea
when simplicity weeps
stupidity grins

Simplicity
is a box of matches
Stupidity
is a forest ablaze
Simplicity
is an egg that hatches
Stupidity
is the murderer's gaze

you ask me
you ask me how I know
I'll tell you

Simplicity came and took my hand
She lead me from the city to a peaceable land
Of complicated creatures and rivers and trees
With days of excitement and nights of peace
And I love the way Simplicity moves
I love the way Simplicity moves

But I have seen enough Stupidity
To last me to the year three thousand and three

Der Bucketspiel

(a little-known and shoddily translated fragment by Brecht's uncle Cecil)

Oh whom did it was invented the bucket?
And whom invented the handle thereof?
And whom did invent the bottom of the bucket
To stand so stern and sturdy on its circle of iron?
And whom did invent that capacious space without a name
Which consists of the hollow interior of the bucket
And which rendered obsolete the solid bucket of our fathers?
Oh whom did it was invented the bucket?
So many questions...so many bloody silly questions...

Cutting It Up

If you're looking for trouble
Here's how to start
Blow up the theatres
Tear down the art

Burn down the libraries
And concert halls
Cut your jazz and ballet
And then cut off your balls
And be a serial killer of culture
A serial killer of the soul

If you're looking for trouble
Take the artists you've got
Stack their works all around them
And torch the lot

The human soul is hungry
And so's the human heart
The food and drink makes them feel and think
It comes from works of art

And the human soul without art
Is locked in a dungeon cell
If you take your knife and cut the arts
You can cut your throat as well
Cos you're a serial killer of culture
A serial killer of the soul

If you're looking for trouble
Cut your grants to the poor
Seek out the old and sick
Cut them some more

Suffer little children
To go to school in Hell
Then watch them burn your cities
And your country estates as well
Cos you're a serial killer of Britain
A serial killer of its soul

THE HAIRY ARTS

The Olchfa Reading

I had told Nigel Jenkins
the bard of Mumbles, who was my friend,
that I wanted to read to a large audience

I was led in to entertain
the fourth and fifth and reject forms
of an enormous comprehensive
in a hall the size of
a Jumbo Jet hangar

They seemed as multitudinous
as the armies of Genghis Khan
but they were larger and hairier
and less interested in poetry

I tried to read a few of my poems –
my political ones were dismissed as ancient history
my love lyrics scoffed at for their naivety
my banter greeted by a thousand embalmed faces

It was a Friday afternoon to end all Friday afternoons
It was Goliath dressed up as Just William
yawning in my face

the audience stretched from Wales to Florida
the front rows shuffled their terrible boots in their sleep
or read magazines with mutilated nudes on their covers

further back they were snorting anthracite
and even further back
they were tearing the blazers off each other's backs
and indulging in Welsh Kissing

Desperately I asked for Questions from the audience.
I've sometimes had good questions
from unpromising aliens, questions like:
how old were you when you turned famous?

But this was bottomless sea-bed of Friday afternoon

A tall boy with several jam-stained
bandages around his head asked me:
Have you got any Horror Poems?
What sort of Horror Poems?
You know, poems with rusty spikes
sticking out of people's necks.
I shook my head – the tall boy snarled
and began to chew one of his bandages

then a lobster-boy in the front row
detached a lump of pink bubble gum from his stubble
before he asked me scornfully:
Why are your trousers so long?

Booze and Bards

I do a lot of thinking stuff all day long
You know trying to chase those words around the page
If I can round up enough of those critters
I might earn a living wage

Every morning down the poetry pit
Cut a few tons from the verseface
But the sky's always darkening by the time
I clamber up to the surface

That's when I run to catch the Jungle Juice Train
Everybody says He's at it again
Well the Jungle Juice Train's what I travel on
To the dear old station of Oblivion

And here's a health to the corpse of Dylan Thomas
And to all of the pain in the poetry dome
He fell among strangers time after time
But he only wanted to be carried home

Bottles of Poetry

Up from the hallowed shadows of his cellars
The Baron rises. His smile promises everything
And his masterly hands cradling
The bottle, that dark tower, that solace.

He fills your glass – bow slightly and inhale –
Silver gardens of medieval roses,
A silky purple fog arises –
Next day your head feels like Cologne Cathedral.

A scruffbin poet bumps you on a bus,
Grins, passes an unlabelled quarter bottle,
Sump oil with a bouquet of rat piddle,
It hits your guts like a rhinoceros.

Comes the dawn – a celestial festival hangover:
You wake in the feathered embrace of a creature,
Who teaches you all the love-dances of flying –
Hilarious Aprilup, Whirling Winghover.

Poet

He swings down from the train
on to the evening platform
the bag bumping his shoulder blade contains
gear for the night and weapons
only the main street shows any brightness
Been here before? Seven years ago.
He leans on the deep gold wood of the bar
orders a double whisky

waiting for the organiser

I've come to clean up this town

Toys for Rich Kids	**Toys for Poor Kids**
Formula One Opera	poetry
Dolphin Bothering	
Cherished Restaurant Tables	
Artistic Necrophilia	

Poetry and Knitting

A good poem and a good sweater
have plenty in common
both keep you warm
but the sweater fits only one person at a time
poem lasts longer

Astrid Furnival
Designed and knitted
A sweater with William Blake on the front
And Catherine Blake on the back
And vice versa
I gave it to Celia
Through heaven and through hell
She wears it for my sake

But this is not typical Contemporary British Knitting
Not at all

There are knitting factories in South East Asia
which produce
Red for Liverpool Blue for Everton
Anything for money scarves

I love the children's mittens which are connected
by a thin woollen rope
which goes up one overcoat sleeve
and down the other
so that the mittens cannot be lost
except by a mixed infant contortionist
with a Stanley knife

I love those knitted dogs
which have trousers and jackets
kind of knitted into them

I love those mighty woollen helmets
hairy all over with a bobble on top
which make toddlers look
like multi-coloured steaming puddings

I love the generously knitted
lop-sided cardigan
with its baggy pockets
smelling of arcane pipe tobaccos –
Old Barty's Green Plug, Parrot Stock,
Cardinal Jasper and Shmoggo's Midnight Toffee

I love the hopeless inspirational
Christmas insanity of an aunt-knitted tie
sent to an aspiring arms salesman
with British Aerospace

I love the shapelessness of woollen slippers
slopping and slapping like two
pink and cosy three-dimensional amoebas

But maybe I don't love
the French knitting of John Ashbery
that just goes on and on
producing one endless knitted turd

Explanation

The poet's briefcase is a plastic bag
the poet's microphone's a hairy eyebrow
through it he broadcasts to the lowbrow and highbrow
The poet's taxi, that's his righthand thumb
the poet's taxi is a souped-up mind
a fourlegged jaguar not the fourwheel kind
the poet's lipstick is a stick of frozen blood
his make up is primeval sludgeration mud
His financial security's an ice cream cone
His political party is called All Alone
There'll be a bill at the end of the meal
Be sure you pay as much as you feel
You only have to pay as much as you feel

He Might Have Looked Better in a Beard

Philip Larkin
Was Chairman of the University of Hull Committee on Parking.
Thinking about and drinking about his own demise
He was like Eric Morecambe without benefit of Ernie Wise.

No Wages for Poets, Please, I Beg You

Ballpoint blood and tears it takes seven cold years
To write one skinny volume for your shelves
But poets are glad to be broke and go mad –
See how picturesquely we top ourselves
Yes poets take the strain and the psychic pain
And the bailiffs – we don't mind a bit –
For we know how the Arts Council values us,
For it pays us in Angel Shit.

The Murder of the Poet Michael Smith
by Three Men in Kingston, Jamaica

You!
You don't belong here.
Why are your walking here?

You!
You don't belong here.
Why are you walking here?

You!
You don't belong here.
Why are you walking here?

I am a free man.
I walk anywhere in this land.

The Wilder Poetry of Tomorrow

Come on Poetry, get up off your big fat rusty-dusty
Come on Poetry, get up off your big fat rusty-dusty
When you crawled home at dawn your breath was smelling
      mausoleum musty

You've been mooning round the boneyard, mumbling to the dead,
Playing Ludo against yourself and wearing gloves in bed
Why don't you swing up through the treetops, get some jungle in
      your head?

I want every kind of creature to break out of the Poetry Zoo –
Barefoot heartbeat of the elephant, stride of the kangaroo.
I want to see your body naked when the sun comes shining through.

It can knock you down in Devon, it can bust you up in Jarrow
It bumps across the landscape like a customised wheelbarrow
But The Wilder Poetry of Tomorrow – it strikes like Robin Hood's
      arrow.

So come on Poetry, get up off your big fat rusty-dusty…

The Collected Poems of Gerald Stimpson, Esq.

A Thought Strikes Gerald Stimpson

Gosh!
I can't wait
  To see
What I'm going to be
  In the
Next Life!

A Jocular Warning from Gerald Stimpson

I say!
Make jolly sure
You don't spell Stimpson
  As Simpson,
Stampson, Stompson
  Or Thompson!

Gerald Stimpson's Satisfactory Day

Wow!
That feels better!
  I weeded the rockery,
  Washed the crockery,
And sorted out the cutlery!
  I deserve a cup of tea!

Gerald Stimpson Reads the Daily Doze

    Good Heavens!
POPE MUCH BETTER.
PRINCESS CALLS OFF DIVORCE.
DERBY WON BY ENGLISH HORSE.
  It's a good warm feeling
    Reading the paper!

Short Back and Sides with a Blowtorch, Please

Barbara Hepworth used to do my hair. I was a weekend Ted in
those days and Miz H could shape a mean Pompadour. She liked
to get a sort of surfer's tunnel through the front, Trough of the
Wave, she called it, and from the right angle you could see right
through my hair like my head had a hole in it, which it didn't. I
jacked in Babs finally because she'd always be playing the Bee Gees
over her salon speakers. Not that she listened to them, she'd be
gabbing in general about different kinds of stone. Stone and rock.
Lizzie Frink used to shampoo me before the cut – it was always a
ten bob tip for Frinkie and a quid for the Hep. They both took it
hard when I switched to Tony Caro's place...Of course the first
barber I went to was old Harry Moore, had a place up the road,
old-fashioned Yorkshire establishment, stick a tripe bowl on your
head and clip around it happily enough whistling Ilkley Moor Ba
Taht or telling stories about driving tube trains during the Blitz.
Naum Gabo once gave me a Yul Brynner...

Movietone News

Next time you watch *The Big Sleep*,
The Maltese Falcon, Casablanca,
Take an extra-deep look at Humphrey Bogart –
His face looks like the sole survivor
Of an aircrash prison riot shipwreck.
The jazz-dark eyes, the husky-whiskey voice,
The total hipness of a leopard
Who has no cool to lose
And the way he walks – like destiny.

Add it all up, and it's obvious,
He passed and very successfully, but
Bogart was black.

And not just Bogey, look at Buster Keaton,
A black angel-dancer
With a face full of the blues –
Buster was black as well.

Of course they had to white up, if they hadn't
All our favourite black movie stars
Would have been condemned to bit parts,
Carrying trays and rolling their eyes –
 James Dean as a squeaky bellhop,
 Clark Gable serving coffees in a Pullman,
 Judy Garland as the superstitious lady's maid,
 Orson Welles as Uncle Tom
And, baring his top row of teeth in a pretence of joy,
The Chattanooga Shoe-Shine Boy –
Bogart, the baddest and blackest of them all, because
Bogart was black, remember, Bogart was black.

For the Next Eurovision Song Contest

Songwriters can't help what they look like
They were born that way more or less
Songwriters can't help what they look like
Boom banga bang boom banga bang bong

Now a ballad is born out of longing
And it blooms like a wonderful rose
But a songwriter's born out of hunger
With spectacles perched on his nose

Hot Pursuit

(to Paul McCartney)

Augusta, Georgia,
Saturday night.
'Car Number Seven
Go break up a fight.'

'Make it downtown
To the Franklin Hotel.
James Brown's in the lobby
And he's kicking up hell.'

James Brown standing
Like a tall black tree.
'Hey little coppers
Did you come for me?'

'Hold it James Brown
Or we're gonna shoot.'
But he took off in a truck,
Law in hot pursuit.

Cop car zooming
Right after James Brown.
He laugh like a jackass
Stuck his foot right down.

'Augusta, Georgia
Is my home town.
Shoot me if you dare
But I'm the famous James Brown.'

'We don't care
If you're the great James Brown.
We'll shoot out your tyres
That'll slow you down.'

Bam! One tyre
Got blown by their first.
Fired another bullet
A second tyre burst.

James Brown, James Brown,
They'll never catch him.
He kept on driving
On the metal rims.

'Catch me alive,
Or catch me dead.
Augusta, Georgia
There's sparkles round my head.'

For William Cowper

Friend of the freezing orange tree
Friend of the slave across the sea
Friend of the kitten and the hare
Friend of the helpless everywhere
Look at our friendless world's distress –
Shine down your golden gentleness

(Written in Cowper's stone summer house at Olney.
He used to call it his 'sulking room' or 'verse manu-
factory'. It is at the end of the second garden behind
Orchard House in the Market Place. I sat there on
30 January 1987. The house contains a painting of
Cowper lighting a fire to keep an orange tree warm in
a night frost and a special door, like a cat-flap, pro-
vided for his pet hares.)

A Unicorn for Salman

There are millions of different living creature on earth.
Millions of different living truths on earth.

It is the job of the artist
To follow the tracks of a living truth,
To find that living truth,
To listen to its songs and watch its dances,
To learn its ways and learn to love it
Until the artist can paint the living truth
And take its image back to his people.

There is a poet called Salman
Who followed the trail of a living truth
And one day stumbled into a glade
Where the living truth stood, grazing quietly.
It was laughing unicorn.
Salman listened to its songs and watched its dances
And learned its ways and how to love it.
And he painted a picture of the unicorn.

It is the job of an artist
To celebrate and sing the living truth.
But there are other people
Whose job is to hunt down the truth
And hack it to death, burn it to death,
Knives, bullets and bombs.
The greater the truth, the greater the danger.
The more beautiful the truth, the more the danger.
Government, churches, corporations, armies –
It is their job to hunt and kill the truth.

It is the job of the artist
To celebrate and sing the unicorn.
It is the job of the unicorn
To bring the blessings of long life and freedom
To her brother, our brother, Salman Rushdie.

Moondog

There was a man called Moondog
Who made tunes
With thimbles, glasses, zithers,
Keys and spoons
And all the tunes he made
Were living things
Which flew around his head
On silver wings

I bought a Moondog record
Fourteen tracks
A red and golden label
Dusty wax
The sounds were delicate
As cowrie shells
The moonlit dancing
Of a thousand bells

My first day in New York
I walked downtown
Moondog sat on the sidewalk
All in brown
He played his instruments
So sweet and wild
I wanted to stay with him
As his child

Deep Purple Wine

Friday in a city
    That was growling with the heat
I saw the tall rain coming
    Walking with a steady beat
It walked right down the sky
    And then scuttled off down the street

Seven in the evening
    Yellow streetlights start to shine
I turned to my woman
    She locked her eyes on mine
She said: Best thing when it's raining
    Is a bottle of Deep Purple Wine

It makes your spirit laugh
    It makes your spirit moan
It makes you feel you're talking to
    An angel on the phone
It cools you then it fools you
    And it warms you to the bone

Duke Ellington invented it
    The greatest ever brew
It was made by Jimmy Blanton
    And by Johnny Hodges too
And it gurgled out with every note
    Old Cootie Williams blew

It tickles like the old pianner
    Mrs Klinkscale taught
It's heavy as the drum-kit
    That Louis Bellson fought
It's light and bright as a kitten
    Or a Billy Strayhorn thought

Tricky Sam Nanton
    Poured it into crazy shapes
Cat Anderson employed it
    In miraculous escapes
Sonny Greer Ray Nance Rex Stewart
    They were all vintage grapes

Don't forget Ben Webster
   Barney Bigard Lawrence Brown
They filled a big cloud with that wine
   And sailed it over town
And every night in Ellington
   That wine came pouring down

Such Sweet Thunder in the throat
   Such a Crescendo In Blue
Black Brown and Beige jump out your cage
   And start Slappin' Seventh Avenue
It Don't Mean A Thing If It Ain't Got That Swing
   Like East St Louis Toodle-oo

So drink to the great Duke Ellington
   And the Deep Purple Wine he made
Deep Purple Wine gives you dancing feet
   Like kangaroos on parade
Deep Purple Wine so fine so fine
   It will never ever fade

Thanks, Duke.

Parade

Have you ever been in Memphis
At midnight Halloween
I been there dad
And it druv me mad
When I saw whut I have seen

There's no city ever was haunted
Like cursed Memphis is
I'd like to tell
About that blue flame hell
So I say with heavy emphasis

There's
Fear in the streets
Fear in the malls
Fear that clutches you
By the balls
There's
Gruesome in the gravy
Grisly in the lemonade
Look what's coming –
Zombie Elvis Presleys on Parade

A million zombie Elvises at the witching hour
hey hey oom borooga boom
A million zombie Elvises twitching with power
hey hey oom borooga boom
Staggering and boogying and woggling their hips
Dropping ears and fingers and noses and lips
A million zombie Elvises
A million zombie Elvises

Oh What a Lovely Man!

Adam and Eve in the Garden of Eden
Friday night and sod-all to do:
The Lord in mercy looked down and told em:
I'll invent The Theatre for you.

So he made the very first dressing room
From a handbag that was dusty and damp
And he said: Let there be stage lighting!
And lo – a carbide bicycle lamp.

And he made a box office from a weetabix box
And a stage from a couple of planks
And he said: Behold the Theatre I've created for you!
And Adam and Eve said: Thanks.

But Eve said: we'll need a Performer
Who can play a Duke a Duck or a Dame.
God said: Let there be a Performer,
And let Brian Murphy be his name.

And Brian Murphy jumped from the dressing-room
To the stage in a single bound
And Adam and Eve felt a shiver of delight
And the Animals gathered round.

For everything he did on that stage was true
And sometimes he hurt Eve's heart
And sometimes he made Adam laugh so much
That his body started flying apart.

And Brian looked at Adam as if figuring out
The cause of this unseemly laughter.
Brian Murphy, with the woebegone face
Of the moon on the morning after.

All the Garden of Eden applauded
And the Lord told Adam and Eve:
Every play will need a Brian Murphy
So the audience will believe.

And whenever there is Brian Murphy
Then all of Creation shall know –
Give him a stage, and lights
And a baggy pair of tights –
And you've got yourself a Show!

And the Lord sang:
One Brian Murphy
There's only one Brian Murphy
One Brian Murphy
There's only one Brian Murphy

And all the Animals sang along:
One Brian Murphy
There's only one Brian Murphy
One Brian Murphy
There's only one Brian Murphy.

Edward Hopper

He found his thing

Cross-legged blondes
waiting quietly

Standing men with sharp grey faces
waiting by doors

People in deckchairs
waiting for the sun to set

And the sun in an empty room
waiting for nobody

He found his thing
he did it

Footnote on the Edward Hopper Exhibition

You just wait there,
says a wife.
Yes, says her husband,
pauses, then shuffles a few steps towards
the raw meat painting called Girlie Show
and stands there, waiting.

The One About Fred Astaire

No
it's
   not so much
     how
he
   moves so much
     so much
       as how he
        stops

and then moves so
   much again all
     over
       every
        anywhere
        all over
          so much

thank you
    Mister Astaire

      so much

Mayakovsky and the Sun
(to Little Richard)

It was the summit of summertime bang in the middle of July.
You could hear the rivers boiling, villages sizzle and fry.
It was that white-hot melting summer that I'll never forget –
The cows came out in blisters and even my sweat had sweat.

The Sun lay in his hammock snoring fit to wake the dead
So I opened up my window and I shouted at him: 'Goldenhead!
My name is Mayakovsky, I'm a poet and a painter too
And I'm doing all I can to make the Revolution come true.'

    Mayakovsky and the Sun...Mayakovsky and the Sun...

'I've been sitting up printing propaganda poems all night
And now it's early morning and I need some poster-painting light
But you're still kipping in your featherbed four-poster cloud!
Get up and get rolling! No layabouts allowed!'

Well the Sun gives a grin and he drags himself up by the roots
And comes marching towards me in his seven-league thumping boots
And he strides through my garden and he bursts into my room
And he opens up his jaws and his lion voice begins to boom:

'Hi Mayakovsky, I turned down my burners for you.
I can see there's a lot in common between us two.
I'd enjoy a conversation, that's the kind of Sun I am –
So where's my favourite glass of tea with cherry jam?'

    Mayakovsky and the Sun...Mayakovsky and the Sun...

I stood there thinking Mayakovsky what the hell have you done?
I was sweating like a waterfall eyeball to eyeball with the Sun.
We shared a bucket of vodka ice cream to cut down the heat
And I said: 'Cosmic Comrade, would you like to take a seat?'

The Sun relaxed back in a rocking chair looking benign
And he said: 'You imagine it's an easy thing for me to shine?
Have a shining competition, you bet I come an easy first.
But if you're going to shine, man, better shine till you burst.'

    Mayakovsky and the Sun...Mayakovsky and the Sun...

Well we talked on and on until the purple began to fall
But the Night didn't dare to stick one toe inside my hall.
When I slapped him on the back the Sun gave a black hole of a yawn
And he said: 'Hey, brother, it's time to do a bit of dawn.

'Let's shine away the boredom of how the everyday world looks.
I'll take care of the sky, Mayakovsky you can take the books.'
So the two of us are kicking down the prison walls built by the Night.
Yes it's a double attack in boots of poetry and light.

So when the Sun shines down, that overworked mate of mine,
That's when I jump up and with all of my spirit I shine.
Shine on! Shine on! Shine on for everyone!
That's what Mayakovsky says, and so does his friend the Sun.

> *Mayakovsky and the Sun...Mayakovsky and the Sun...*

The One Good Poster

Pacific blueness, pasteurised mountain snows,
The ultimate sports car like a pink toenail,
Oily brown basted shoulders
And all the happy gas of holiday hoardings
Told me: Buy sex. Buy speed.
Buy rank. Buy cancer.
Stand and deliver your money or your life.

All but one. Pasted to a car-park fence.
A crow-black woodcut on rough cream paper,
Pictures and letters coloured in by hand
With luminous water colours.
It was the size of a shove-ha'penny board.
It glowed like a shove ha'penny board.

The good poster said to me:
BE SURE YOU ASK
FOR BEALE'S IMAGINARY LIST.

The Perils of Reading Fiction

If you read too many books with made-up stories you go a bit mad
That's what my Sergeant used to say every time he saw anyone
      reading
All those writers, most of them foreign and dead,
With their freaky ideas and nancy ways and gone with the
      how'syourfather
All those Swish Family Robinsons and Lorna Dooms and King
      Falstaffs
And The Great Fatsby and Virginia Beowulf and Kubla Khan-Khan
And Jane Austen and Jane Morris and Jane Volkswagen
All of em jumbled up and tripping over each other in your brainbox
Well it's like letting a year's worth of dreams out of a corrall
To stampede all over your real life, all those pretty lies and ugly lies,
Whirling about inside your skull, beating up storms of yellow dust
So soon you can't see for the grit in the eyes, you can't look out at all
And see the real world which is just the real world
And is real and not made up by somebody trying to be clever –
Listen – what I say is –
If you read too many books with made-up stories you go a bit mad.

Looking Down and Looking Down

sure I can look down at an old scratched brown wooden tabletop
and see a swarm of battling and journeying, loving and flying creatures
in landscapes with moving mountains and solid seas
and I can look down through the surface of that table
upon my denim shorts and hairy knees
and I can look down there extending my range
and see beneath my sandals
a blackdeep well where crocodiles circle
illuminated by Roman candles
I stare through the tons of water in the well
and the soakedbaked clay of its base
to see the sapphire eyes of a woman
smile from her muddy face
but looking further I can only see
a crimson pulse about to burst in birth
which may be really back behind my eyes
or maybe at the centre of the earth

COUNTRY LIFE

Dart River Bed

The mash of rotted-down oak leaves
of bark from drifting branches
the white flesh blackening of the salmon
who jumped the net and perished of old age
under her shadow-rock
the ragged robin chewed into shreds
the rich rust of a radiator
the bones of voles polished down to white specks
the dragged down muslin
robbed of its dye then mashed to filaments
and sweet Ophelia too –

all in the soft cool deeps of mud
under the mirror
all in the soft cool deeps of mud
all one in the soft cool deeps of mud

gradually dancing down to the ocean

That June

most days the sun was friendly
a few showers of fat warm raindrops
life was a hammock slung between the trees
of birth and death

poetry was a glass of iced tea
with a submerged seeping lemon slice
the silver condensation
singing in my palm
such easy days such easy days
I didn't think all month

You gave me a perfect cherry
I bit it ate it and spat the stone
all the way to St Petersburg
where it hit Pushkin on the nose
and he began to laugh
that June

The Rain in June

Soggy cardboard skies.

I was on all fours
Counting the gravel.

A man drove up
In a two-litre bottle of Slimmer's Lemonade.

His face was at my ear
Like a wet flannel.

He said: 'You can go home now –
But you won't recognise it.'

A Million Daisies

The woods are littered with breakfast cereal
Carefully the sun pours yellow milk
Down the long gardens dance the ghosts of roses
over the whitewater rapids of a million daisies

November on the Hill

birds, the raucous and the sweet,
circle the blue roof of the wood
demonstrating against the cold,
while the last butterflies
like blessings
skim on the little thermals rising from
the greying, thirsty grass.

Winter Listening

Humble, crumbly song of the snails.
Pinecones rattling in a stormy tree.
The frosty voices of December stars.
Dragon-roaring of a factory.

Honking slapstick of seals at play.
The creak and slish of snow off a roof.
Crackle-whisper of Christmas paper.
The silver step of a unicorn's hoof.

Winter Night in Aldeburgh

I stood beside the dark white tower
and fancied I heard a train over in Holland

There was an old man keeping himself warm
by leaning against the fish and chip shop wall

out of the corner of my left eye –
a gang of grey cats pedalling miniature bicycles

an orange boiled sweet sat stuck to the pavement
it was the size and shape of a rugby ball
and was bleeding orange sugar

I looked into the boating pond
and the boating pond looked into me
enough – I saluted the enormous moon
and scuttled back into my room

every inch of this town is haunted I said to myself
but I don't mind these ghosts
they have no business with me

at this moment a newsaper thrust itself through my letter-box
and fell on the mat with a sound like salt being poured
it was the ghosts' gazette, the newspaper
which is published by the dead for the dead

at first it was like reading a gravestone
covered with silver moss
but then I started to make out the words

The headline read
OCEAN INVASION ALERT
and the story began:
A squadron of green-headed mermen is swimming shorewards
through the torn metal desert of the waves
towards the singing shingle.

Now I am lying in my bed
face down eyes shut
I am awaiting instructions from the dead

Two Old Ladies Overheard in Totnes

awful when it happens to someone so young
   so young
It's a terrible thing
      terrible thing
terrible
You don't know what to say, do you
   You don't know what to say
Cos really and truly there's nothing you can say is there
   No there's nothing

If a thing is worth having, it's worth waiting for

The Monster's Dream

Under the shoulder of Mount Ferocity
The fugitive monster's head hums itself to sleep
And he steps out of his head into a fresh dream –

And the air in his fresh dream is chilly-blue
Feathers falling flowers spiralling upwards
Brown tarns shouting as waterbirds skid on their waterskins

The dew on the grass is a moon of crystal frost
Tickling the dark soles of the monster's feet
And the sun is mild and white and far away

It is early in the morning it is early in the world
All the bad warriors have sailed off to their hero fortresses
Or fallen over the edge of the world

It is early in the morning it is early in the heart
As the fugitive monster breaks through the bracken to find
The ghost of his mother sitting in the grass
Her monster face all gentle for love of him

The Interrupted Nap

I wake with a terrible shock. I feel
That I might be, possibly, missing a meal!

4.25 pm January 1st 1993

Put Your Brain to Bed

You've done it again
You've been thinking with your brain
It's burning and buzzing and tight
Put your brain to bed
And tell it a story
And then tuck it up for the night

A Living Monument
(for Peter, Cathy and Thom Kiddle)

Raised myself a monument – somewhere way back there.
Most people miss it. They move too fast.
It crouches in the little grass, snuffling the blue air,
      A deep-eyed animal, bred to last.

I'll die, but that much of me will keep on lurking,
Not rusting into mudweeds like Cleopatra's barge,
But alive to the beat of the planet, songbark working
      While there's one rocker still at large.

My verses will afterburn, like a good curry,
Though Penguins turn their back on them and BBC TV
And Buckingham Palace and Esher, Surrey –
            But some schoolkid'll learn them, secretly.

Some children love some of my poems – and that's enough!
That was why I bled all over the page.
In a smooth country my songs were a bit rough
            Praising gentleness in a vicious age.

My poetry's an old border collie who gets by
Performing tricks or rounding up the sheep
And it'll keep digging as long as politicians lie
            And mothers weep.

(after Horace, Derzhavin and Pushkin)

When the Dapple is on the Chapel
I Take a Pint of Gerard Manley Hopkins
and Other Country Lore
(for Cicely and Ian Herbert)

            Red sky in the North
The favourite comes fourth
            Red sky in the South
Not a creature is stirring not even a mouth

            Red sky in the West
Shepherd undressed
            Red sky in the East
Shepherdess not interested in the least

            Red sky in the South West
Shepherd fails *One Man and His Dog* screen test
            Red sky on the hills
Shepherd's valium pills

Red sky on the cottage
Shepherd had up for frottage

Red sky at dusk
Shepherds' discussion group

Syllables of Wasted Time

slow anger
slow wrath
unroll from my stomach
as a crimson path

and by the edge
of the pathway lie
a crumpled Tuesday
a broken July

a fruit-tree bright with blossom
gone to crunchy ash
good times turned by money
to a heap of poison trash

slow anger
slow rage
where there should have been an image of angel diving
another torn-out page

Another Attempt at a Nature Poem, But Don't Worry, Ted

The vixen springs
The sparrow sings
The mole grins in his trap
The eagle swings
Her brazen wings
The bunny has a crap

SOME ANIMALS

Bird Dreaming

(for Roger Woddis)

And in my dream a little shaking cloud
Of ten-eleven-twelve birds kept me company
As I ambled beside the chalky ploughed-up fields
And the clear frosty skies watched over me.

So I whistled a Hoagy Carmichael tune
And called the birds with outstretched arm.
One starling landed on my scarlet thumb,
Pressing its stars into my palm.

I kissed the feathers of its breast
And said: Some of them are beginning to know me.
And I felt the warmth of that bird's heart
And my own heart was fiery.

Little Grey

     learn to sit by me
little grey cat
     nowhere is safer
than my corduroy lap

Sausage Cat

Behold the cat
the cat full of sausage
his ears do slope backwards
his coat's full of glossage

His whiskers extend
like happy antennae
he would count his blessings
but they are too many

He unfoldeth his limbs
he displayeth his fur
he narrows his eyes
and begins to purr

And his purring is smooth
as an old tree's mossage
Behold the cat
who is full of sausage.

A Cat Called Slumber

In the middle of the night appears
My day-shy tabby with collapsable ears
And I stroke her head so those ears collapse
And she purrs to say that she loves me, perhaps...

Epitaph for a Golden Retriever

It was my job
To be a dog

My master said
That I was good

Now I turn myself around
And lie down in the musky ground

For Golden Ella

At four in the morning
With furry tread
My good dog climbs
Aboard my bed

She lays her chin
In my open palm
Now neither of us
Can come to harm

In my open hand
Her long jaw seems
Like a shifting weight
As she chews at her dreams

From the coolness
Of her nose
The blessing of
Her breathing glows

And the bad night
Vampires disappear
As my wrist is tickled
By her ear

Elegy for Number Ten
(for Ella)

One out of ten, six gold, four black,
Born in a bulging transparent sack.

I eased him out, this holy gift.
His mother turned to him and sniffed

Then licked the blood and the sack away.
All small and golden, there he lay.

There are some insects and some flowers
Whcse life is spent in twenty-four hours.

For twenty-four hours, beside his mother,
He fed and he slept with his sisters and brothers.

Good smells. Close warm. Then a crushing weight.
Then nothing at all. His head the wrong shape.

He was wrapped up and taken beyond the bounds
Of his mother's familiar digging grounds

For she would have found him and known him too
And have wept as golden retrievers do.

So she kept all her love for the alive –
The black four and the golden five.

But I celebrate that golden pup
Whom I talked to and kissed as I wrapped him up

For he fed and he slept and was loved as he lay
In the dark where he spent one golden day.

Now his mother pursues an eccentric trail
With casual sweeps of her lavish gold tail

And when number ten stumbles into my mind
She consoles me and so do the other nine.

The Meaningtime

Bananas and bicycles are beautiful animals
Elephants and waterfalls are wonderful machines
Show me a bucket and I'll bite you a biscuit –
Now you know what the universe means

Understanding the Rain
(for a horse called Elgin)

Top right-hand corner
Of a South Devon field
The great white horse
Stands under the warm rain

Slow-motion grass
Growing greener and greener
The great white horse
Stands under the warm rain

Like a shining cathedral
Under the centuries
The great white horse
Stands under the warm rain

Like a waiting messenger
Like the people
Like the planet
Like poetry
Like a great white horse
The great white horse
Stands under the warm rain

A Cheetah, Hunting

A herd of Thompson's Gazelle
Like 43 bars of marzipan.

The great wheels of the cheetah's shoulders.
The black tracks of her killer tears.

And now her teeth are in a throat.

Two huge lakelight eyes
Look upwards with such love.

Here Come the Bears

Clambering through the rocky torrents
Here come the bears
Quicksilver salmon flip into the light
to flop a little higher up
swerving past scooping claws
and underwater gaping muzzles
to flip up into the light again
past the black tip
of the nose of a small bear
his eyes as wide as all amazement

The Elephant

Elephant Elephant
Simmering gently
Carry me home
As smooth as a Bentley

Elephant Eternity

Elephants walking under juicy-leaf trees
Walking with their children under juicy-leaf trees
Elephants elephants walking like time

Elephants bathing in the foam-floody river
Fountaining their children in the mothery river
Elephants elephants bathing like happiness

    Strong and gentle elephants
    Standing on the earth
    Strong and gentle elephants
    Like peace

Time is walking under elephant trees
Happiness is bathing in the elephant river
Strong gentle peace is shining
All over the elephant earth

JOIN THE POETRY
AND SEE THE WORLD

Blue Coffee

Blue coffee
The air was like
Blue coffee

Frothy cow's parsley
Either side of the path
Across the Heath

Blue coffee
The whirling air was like
Blue coffee

Up jumped a poppy in scarlet
Her heart beating black as the blues

Blue coffee
The swirling, spiralling air
Blue coffee

Vauxhall Velvet

After-dark London crouches
Like a grisly grimy cat
The Funman slouches
Underneath the bridge in his fuck-you hat
As the pedestrians go skulking home,
Each skull a fragile stained-glass dome.

Frome Pomes

(Written during two workshops at Frome Community College on 27 January 1994)

Monowheel Rejoicing

A wheelbarrow
On a grass ski-slope!
Pass me my pen
And my wheelbarrow jotter!
Oh wow is me!
Oh jubilee!
I am a happy Wheelbarrow Spotter!

Sad Carpet

Poets and mud
Attract each other
For poets know
Mud was our Mother
Great things are done
When mud and poets meet
Then we jump up and down
To get the mud off our feet

Thursday Breeze

Red wine jacket and black skirt
Her eyes are searching the tree-tops
As the wind writes poems in her hair

By the Waters of Liverpool

So many of her sons drowned in the slime of trenches
So many of her daughters torn apart by poverty
So many of her children died in the darkness
So many of her prisoners slowly crushed in slave-ships
Century after red century the Mersey flowed on by –
By the waters of Liverpool we sat down and wept

But slaves and the poor know better than anyone
How to have a real good time
If you're strong enough to speak
You're strong enough to sing
If you can stand up on your feet
You can stomp out a beat...

So we'd been planning how to celebrate
That great red river of Liverpool
As our team rose to a torrent
That would flood the green of Wembley
We'd been planning how to celebrate
The great red dream of Liverpool
For Dalglish held the Cup in his left fist
And the League in his right –
By the waters of Liverpool we sat down and wept

Our scarves are weeping on the gates of Anfield
And that great singing ground is a palace of whispers
For the joy of the game, the heart of the game,
Yes the great red heart of the great red game
Is broken and all the red flowers of Liverpool –
By the waters of Liverpool we sat down and wept.

April 1989, after Hillsborough

Swansea Triplets

Hotel Comradeship

A dove on my windowsill
Both of us gazing
And cooing at each other

Posh Swansea Pub

My Muse is on the juke-box
Work With Me Baby
I open my red notebook

Swansea Waterfront

Words scribbled on dark waters
Illuminated
By the feathered light of swans

Night Thoughts in Swansea

in my glassy globe head
soap-flake snow sinks down
like my thoughts in this
precarious town

I'm transfixed by one place-name
on the Swansea map
which lies like a white wing
across my lap

and I stand in my swirling
glassy-skull dome
an inmate of
The Lost Animal Home

In the Queen's Hotel, Swansea

The big man bursts into song:
Please Don't Talk About Me When I'm Gone.
He sits there, singing along
With the juke-box flashing inside his head
Purple and red all round its whirling turntable.

He waves his two huge hands in front of him
From side to side like meaty wings.
His two ladies smile and giggle around them
And their blouses bulge with pride
To be at the big man's table
While the big man sings.

Night Thoughts in Treorchy

Shakespeare should have stayed in Stratford upon Avon
and written about Warwickshire
not Italian teenagers up to no good
or alien lovers in imaginary woods
or a black soldier having a hard time in the army
or a Danish Prince gradually going barmy

He should have stuck to Stratford subjects
and the Stratford problems of Stratford folk
You can say my mind's narrow
but it runs in a clean little groove
It goes round and round
for I have found
that's the safest way to move
call me a bigot but for my part
I don't want aliens from Outer Art.

I Am Tourist

I am Tourist
I fly across the seas with a cold glass in my hand
Watching Burt Reynolds movies
I am Tourist
With my chocolate-coloured spectacles
And my blue travellers chequetacles
And my video camera purring at the Sights
I am Tourist
With my Tourist Wife
We live the full and beautiful
Tourist Life
We are taken to a hill tribe
They live on a hill
They sell us many boxes
Painted green and grey
They are ugly boxes but very inexpensive
Then they put on hairy masks
And scarlet knickerbockers
They bang their stomachs and circle round us
Is it a wedding? Is it a funeral?
Whatever it is we video it all
And it is picturesque but it is not inexpensive
On the way back to the hotel
I tell our Guide
No more painted boxes
No more picturesque ceremonies
No more hill tribes
I want a mattress
And a pool and a bar
Just like back home
I am Tourist

March in Vienna

March in Vienna
March in Vienna
Coffee Danke Schoen that's one tenner

London in March

London in March
London in March
Where the wind whistles round your Marble Arch

The Postman's Palace

Deep down in France is the village of Hauterives,
A village as quiet
As a heap of stones by the roadside...
To the brave heart, nothing is impossible.

A new postman came to Hauterives
And he was known as Le Facteur Cheval
Which means, in English, Postman Horse.
Time does not pass, but we do.

One night Postman Horse dreamed himself a dream
And in it he saw, at the bottom of his garden,
A wonderful palace of stairways and towers
Decorated with trees and fruit made of stone
And camels and giants and goddesses and elephants.
Out of art, out of a dream, out of energy.

Next day Postman Horse was on his rounds
When he tripped over an odd-shaped stone.
He took it home in his wooden wheelbarrow,
Set it on the ground in his garden, and smiled.
This is where the dream becomes reality.

Postman Horse began to build.
Every day on his rounds he found amazing stones.
Every day after work he collected them.
Carefully, each evening, he cemented the stones together.
Gradually the palace of his dreams began to rise.
To the brave heart, nothing is impossible.

After ten thousand days of work
In the freezer of winter, the oven of summer,
After thirty-three back-breaking years of work
The palace was finished.
Postman Horse wrote on panels of cement:
All that you see as you pass by
Is the work of a peasant,
The work of one man alone.
Time does not pass, but we do.

I have seen the palaces
Of the Kings of England, France and Russia.
They were magnificent and dead.
But deep down in France is the village of Hauterives
And from its earth there rises
A wonderful palace built out of dreams
Where Postman Horse inscribed these words:

To the brave heart, nothing is impossible.
Time does not pass, but we do.
Out of art, out of a dream, out of energy.
This is where the dream becomes reality.

Julie's House in Deya

Lemon trees lemon trees
Singing their hearts out all night
As I lay reading Charlotte Brontë
By their lemon light

Lerici, The Bay, Early on Saturday, May

orchards awash
with rippling green shadow

a buttercup schoolbus
blurts its trumpet at me

an Egyptian lion of an island
dozily gazes
at a warm breadroll of an island

by and by, says the lion,
I will eat you,
by and by

and now, like a slow-motion dancer
in a crimson dress
with a white neckline
a trawler lies in the middle of the blue stage
waiting for the opening music
of the Shelley ballet

the words of Shelley's spirit
dance like the flames round a gas ring

strong and painful and transparent
and hot enough to melt the heart of England

pass round that bottle of blue flames
let's drink to Shelley

The British School at Rome
(for Charlotte and William)

Below a carving of deer in flight
Lies a pool shaped like the letter O.
The largest possible goldfish
Swoops along in his gangster suit.

He ate up all the children's tadpoles.
Big fish, I say to him,
Big fish – pig-fish!

Helsinki Statue Notes

Cloudberry-juiced to the Senate Square
Poets and Czars were everywhere
Amanda sat among four barking seals
I hope she's not as cold as she feels

Peace Memories of Sarajevo

Sarajevo glowing white
as a translucent china cup

Sarajevo forty poets in suits on an official platform
Reciting eight lines each under a giant portrait of Tito

Sarajevo my daughter aged eight laughing
As she stands in the concrete rain-filled
Footsteps of the assassin

Sarajevo in the smoky little orchards on the hills
Families sitting under gentle-eyed blossoms
Enjoying their slow dinners

Sarajevo and my brave schoolmaster friend
Who did not blink when the bureaucrats spat in his eye

Sarajevo I wish you no bombs no shells no guns
I wish you smoky little orchards and glowing poets
And soldiers who refuse to kill
And children who refuse to kill

And Sarajevo
Glowing white
As a translucent china cup

For My Friends in Georgia

The good old moon drank a bottle of wine
And she began to sing

The fine old tree drank a bottle of wine
And he began to sing

The warm black sea drank a bottle of wine
And she began to sing

The strange old bridge drank a bottle of wine
And it began to sing

The tattered little book drank a bottle of wine
And it began to sing

The dog with one ear drank a bottle of wine
And he began to sing

And the child
With a broken doll in his arms
Drank a breastful of milk
And she began to sing

For the love of Georgia
For the love of Georgia
A land with a heart as big
As the good old wine drinking moon

New York

in the shadow of the towers of Troy
Helen brought my cheeseburger – 'Enjoy!'

Which Do You Want? The Truth Or the Treacle?

I explored the alien city
From threatening North
Down to sneering South
And then I caught
The bus back home
And took my thumb
Out of my mouth.

One Week of Hell on SR 2

(The Police Report column from the Monroe Monitor/Valley News, *serving Monroe, Sultan and the Skykomish Valley, near Seattle, Washington, USA, 6th May 1987.)*

County Sheriff's Report

On Monday a fight was reported on Moonlight Drive near Gold Bar. A man was fighting with a male friend of his ex-girlfriend.

A Skyco Drive resident near Index reported someone had stolen the CB radio from his car. He'd left it parked and unlocked for several days.

On Tuesday an East Tester Road man was arrested on simple assault charges. He had been drinking, and became involved in a fight with his wife and mother.

On Wednesday a 249th Avenue South East man was arrested on simple assault charges. A 50-year-old man fought with his 50-year-old friend because the friend had tried to kiss his mother.

Monroe Police Report

On Monday a motor-cycle was reported parked in a yard on Oak Street. Police found the motor-cycle parked in the street.

A group of kids was reported at a parking lot on SR 2.

On Wednesday police were asked to check the welfare of a Fremond Street resident and found he was okay.

On Thursday police assisted county police search for a suspicious person on 195th Street South East. The area checked clear.

Someone punched holes in a wall in a vacant residence on Elizabeth Street.

Police stood by while a person removed a bed from a Killarney Circle residence.

A window was broken at a South Lewis Street store. Nothing was missing.

A woman reported a man followed her into a Lewis Street store. He told her he was supposed to pick her up and take her east. She told him he was mistaken. Another woman reported he had followed her as well. The man was last seen waiting for a bus out of town.

On Friday a woman was reported crying at a store on SR 2. She got in a car as a passenger. Police stopped the car and found she was involved in a domestic argument.

A disabled vehicle reported on 179th Street South East was gone when police arrived.

A Charles Street resident reported he found his car door open.

A suspicious vehicle reported on West Main Street turned out to be a firefighter taking a nap.

Police impounded a Collie-mix dog at Kelsey and Main Streets.

On Saturday a woman at a residence on SR 2 reported a trespasser. She entered her daughter's residence to find her daughter's ex-boyfriend in the home. She asked police to remove the man, as the rent was paid in her name.

A 149th Street South East woman reported she'd left her dog inside and came home to find the dog outdoors.

A woman and children were reported taking topsoil from a lot on SR 2. The woman said she had the owner's permission.

A prowler was reported looking into windows on North Street.

Someone kicked a hole in a fence on Pike Street.

On Sunday a Fremont Street resident reported someone knocking on the door.

A car parked on Buck Island turned out to be a driver catching a nap.

A West Columbia resident reported someone scratched the paint on a truck parked outside.

Sultan Police Report

The Sultan police report is unavailable from Sultan police.

Gold Bar Police Report

The Gold Bar police report is unavailable from Gold Bar police.

From an English Phrase Book

Wake me with champagne and scrambled eggs, waiter,
Just before we cross the Equator.

Don't Call Us

Stalin phoned Pasternak's
Noisy flat.
'Hello, Boris.'
'Er – hello – can we chat?'

'What about?' asked Stalin.
The poet said:
'Life and death.'
The phone went dead.

When the Government

When the government whips
when the government whips
it's a special kind of gangster
bashing out its brutal will
with a mouthful of morality
heartful of cruel thrill

When the government kills
when the government kills
it's a special kind of murderer
strangling with a hypocrite's sigh
mouthful of deterrence
heartful of hang shoot and fry

When the government tortures
when the government tortures
it's a special kind of thug
who's trained to be a terrorcop
mouthful of security
heart full of poison to the top

When the government bombs
when the government bombs
it's a special mass murderer
crazy with its own success
mouthful of democracy
worldful of emptiness

Twenty-one Haikus

Gales sweep the garden –
In the January sun
A sack relaxes.

Icarus is back –
He survived a thousand flights
In that fedora.

I have a green pen.
It is a Japanese pen.
It writes blue English.

We invited all
The local poultry to dine
And served them omelettes.

Haiku? Too easy.
Everyone knows poetry
Should be difficult.

Retsina so cold
It misbehaves like ice cream
In my sinuses.

Down Mount Pleasant's slopes
The women roll, like marbles,
Their china-blue eyes.

Ace, King, Queen, Jack, Ten –
That's an unbeatable hand!
But this is football.

Fifty plus – you feel
You're being followed by him –
The shadow-faced man.

Path hot in the sun.
It pauses in a little wood –
A shadow-shower.

Five, seven and five
Is the form the haiku takes –
Unlike the warthog.

> The teenage husband
> Using his new wife's toothpaste –
> Ah! Tastes of ice cream.

Thumb, fingers and hand
Picked up a stone, threw it up –
It landed on fist.

> Gold-moss morning path –
> A brown-faced squirrel jumps
> Over a starling.

Mirrors shine, mirrors
Shine, mirrors shine, mirrors shine –
Why are they shining?

> Dropped from Sorrow Trees,
> Tears bob along the river
> Like October pears.

Chuck Berry was changed
To a pink Cadillac by
The Pepsi Fairy.

> Jerry Lee Lewis
> Built himself a cathedral
> Of Budweiser cans.

Buddy Holly's soul
Hitchhiked a ride to Heaven
In a Cloud V8.

> Duke Ellington won
> The Battle of Wonderloo
> With smooth volcanoes.

When the pain's too bad
She brings the black medicine.
Death is a kind nurse.

The Boy Who Danced with a Tank

It was the same old story
Story of boy meets State
Yes the same old story
Story of boy meets State
The body is created by loving
But a tank's made of fear and hate

Armoured cars and heads in helmets
Rank on rank on rank on rank
The hearts of the soldiors were trembling
But the eyes of the soldiers were blank
And then they saw him swaying –
The boy who danced with a tank

The tank moved left
The boy stepped right
Paused like he was having fun
The tank moved right
The boy stepped left
Smiled at his partner down the barrel of its gun

You remember how we watched him
Dancing like a strong young tree
And we knew that for that moment
He was freer than we'll ever be
A boy danced with a tank in China
Like the flower of liberty

Sweet Point Five Per Cent

I saw my Iraqi sister
There was red stuff running from her eyes
She said My son is dying in a hospital
With no medical supplies.
I said Well you shouldn't have started that war
Does he really need an oxygen tent?
But I was feeling generous so I took my week's wages
And slipped her point five per cent.

I bumped into my African brother
The bones were pushing through his skin
He was carrying a skeleton baby
In a coffin hammered out of tin
Well both my kids are at public school
And I have to pay my mistress's rent
Plus my motoryacht and an island I've got –
Still I chucked him point five per cent.

I met my Indian mother
She was staggering through iron rain
She said The Earth turned into a monster
Eating everything we had all that's left is pain.
Now I believe that charity begins at home
And home in my case is Kent.
But before I drove away in my Jaguar
I threw my mother point five per cent.

I drove on and on playing Elton John
But I lost control on a curve
And I failed to see a stupid great tree
And I didn't have time to swerve.
The next thing I saw was St Peter at the Gates
And I asked him where should I go?
You'll spend point five per cent of your time in Heaven
Ninety-nine point five per cent down below.

Shanty Town Song

Sand and dust
Earth's poor sisters
Faces pale yellow and dirty grey

Sand and dust
Playing together
In the blue wind of a winter day

> They chased each other
> Between the shacks
> With red tin roofs
> And window-sacks
> They raced each other
> Past the medicine hut
> But they scrambled and fell and turned into mud
> In a water-filled rut

Sand and dust
Are happier now
Because they put first things first

Better survive
In a stinking dark ditch
Than roam free and die of thirst

The Lion Dancers

The spicy breezes of a Singapore evening
tickle the skin
of the lapis lazuli swimming pool
and all that jadey surface giggles.

As I wrote the word giggles a tinpan band erupted
wiping away the drizzle of muzak
and I saw two cheerful purple lions
shaking their orchid petal fur
stomping their glee at some glumbum businessmen

and the lion band kept cooking, so good and tinny
Sounded like home
Sounded like a hardware store with shining dustbins dancing
a hardware store staggering in a typhoon
Sounded like the pots and pans of a Chinese kitchen
in a funky earthquake
Sounded like – it's only wok and spring roll
but I like it –
and suddenly it clattered to a halt
and the drizzle of muzak dribbled again

and off went the purple lion heads and the jolly Lion Dancers
and the bash clash bash of their party was no more
and the best sound I ever heard in Singapore
the shaking rattling roll of the purple lion's roar.

Ten Holes for a Soldier

Two holes were the size of the holes in his ears.
They were rounded, and as they opened and shut
They seemed to make a sound like sighing.

Two holes were the size of his nostrils,
Close together and dark inside
And breathing out a smell of something – rotting.

Two holes were the size of his eyes
And they were trying to clench themselves
To hold back – the red tears.

One hole was the size of his mouth
And it cried out
Wlth the voice of – an old child.

One hole was the size of the hole
In the end of his cock
And it was skewered by a white-hot, turning gimlet.

One hole was the size of the hole in his arse,
Small and wincing away from the light
And it went – very deep.

Petrol was poured into all his holes.
All of his holes were set on fire.

They covered his holes with a clean uniform.
They flew him home. There was a flag.
In the village he loved, they put him in a hole.

Old Man in Swains Lane

There's a dewdrop on the end of his nose that the sun comes
         shining through.
He wears tennis shoes discarded by Tennyson at the Zoo in '82.
His toes have corns like yellow volcanoes and his ears are tarmac
         blue
But his mind is a crystalline palace and it's dedicated to you.

YOUNG AND OLD

My Father and Mother *or* Why I Began to Hate War

My father was small and quiet, with a brown face
And lines of laughter round his eyes
And wildly sprouting Scottish eyebrows.
Everybody called my father Jock.
In 1914 he joined the army.
He fought for four years in the mud of the trenches.

Nearly all his friends were killed in that war.
He told me about one friend of his
Who suddenly, in the lull between bombardments,
Fell on all fours, howled like an animal,
And was never cured.
My father was a small and quiet man.

My mother was called Kay.
She had blue eyes and a comical nose
And a doll called Beauty.
And she had two older brothers
Called Sydney and Stanley.
Sydney was dark and Stanley was fair
And they used to pull my mother's long gold plaits –
And she loved them dearly.

In 1914 Sydney joined the army
And was killed within days.
Next year Stanley went to the war
To take revenge for his brother.
But Stanley was killed as well.

In 1918 my father came home
With a sword and a kilt and shrapnel in his arm
And Jock and Kay met and fell in love
At the Presbyterian Badminton Club.

And in good time they had two sons
And one of us was dark and one was fair.
And I think, in a way, my brother James and I
Came here to take the place of Sydney and Stanley
My mother's two beloved brothers.

And when I think about war I remember
How when Remembrance Day came round each year,
My mother always wore two poppies.

Childhood Memories

In all the streams
running down into the millstream
there were sticklebacks,
tailbacks of sticklebacks

Rainbow Woods

I was nearly seven when war broke out.
My brother James and I were evacuated
To Combe Down, a village of bright stone
on the hill above the city of Bath.
My friends and I were always being chased
out of farmland and parkland and private estates.
Boys Keep out. Trespassers Will Be Executed.
Till we found a free place, Rainbow Woods.

Rainbow Woods, as bright as a paint-box,
Packed with steep hills and curving pathways,
A switchback speedway
Buzzing with kids on bikes,
Scooting over the roots,
Whirring and whirling through the air
To crash-land in bushes.

Running kids, climbing kids,
Kids crawling under heaps of autumn leaves,
Kids with dogs and calapults
Totally ignored by the grown-up world.

Rainbow Woods
With a thousand trees
And a hundred hills.
Rainbow Woods
With its mysterious ruin
Like a palace for ghosts...

The Bully

His head was a helmet
His muscles sprung steel
Each finger was
An electric eel
He was merciless
As the Bloody Tower
I was eight years old
And I was in his power

To the Sadists of My Childhood

old fear
old fear
got it up to here
boiling white
through my guts
old fear

old fear
old fear
screaming in my ear
holding tight
to my balls
old fear

eight year
seven year
six year
five year old terrors
tearing me apart
they ripped my arsehole
sewed up my lips
and they froze my heart

old fear
old fear
took my mother away
left me in the grip
of old fear
old fear

Putsborough Sands

At the seaside my brother and I took flight.
We leapt down the sand-dunes in giant strides
Like the god Mercury with wings on his heels
And we called this sandhill flying – Mercurying.

The wonderful freedom of limitless sand...
We constructed intricate systems of canals
To feed the enormous dams we built
Out of rocks and sand, dams that filled and filled
Till we could stand waist-deep in their waters.

The wonderful freedom – and safety too,
For our brown-faced father sat at the end
Of a distant rock fishing peacefully
While our mother dozed in her deckchair or read
Biographies with her blue eyes through blue spectacles.
We were free we were safe, you could call it peace...

Peace was a banana milk-shake in a café.

Putsborough beach where I first fell in love.
I remember the moment. I was fourteen.
Her dark hair was flowing over her freckles.
She stood barefoot in her turquoise dress,
Then her brown arms swung
And the bat in her hand smashed the rounders ball
And also my heart, way into the distance.

And I loved her silently for four years
And wrote eight hundred midnight poems for her
Which I was ashamed to show to my dog...

Making Poison Gas

One day, with our Number Four Chemistry Set,
My brother and I made a poison gas
Which the Instruction Leaflet warned us
Could be dangerous for children.

It was a dark green, smoky liquid
And it seethed in its glass jar
Like an imprisoned demon.
James was older, so he took first sniff.
Nothing, he said, we've got it wrong.
I took a small sniff: Nothing, I said,
That can't be gas.
James lowered his nose into the jar
And took an enormous sniff,
A proper snoutful.

And then he stood up
And then he was white
And then he was dark green
And then he began to vomit
And kept on vomiting for twelve hours
Until he was rid of the chlorine gas
Which was one of the kinds of poison gas
Used in my father's war.

But we still thought war was a game
Of Dinkey toy tanks
And bang bang films
Full of Nazi devils
Versus the Spitfire angels of the RAF.

My first air raid.
And I stood on the doorstep
Shaking with excitement in a blanket
At the searchlights and ack-ack fire
And the whine of bombers and the far
Thud of the bombs on Bath.
But next morning we saw a real family
Standing with a few suitcases
Outside what had been their home
Now shattered and blackened by a real-life bomb.
It was then I knew war was more than a game.

Spitfire Daydream

The loudspeaker shouted: 'Scramble'
Downing my Tizer I ran across the tarmac
And vaulted into the cockpit
Of my personal Spitfire
As its props whirled into an ear-burning blur
And the trusty mechanic in baggy overalls
Pulled away the chocks and my Spitfire sprinted forward
And back came the joystick and I was up through the clouds
Leading the V formation of my flight
Over Kent and looking down
To see Jerry bombers over the white cliffs
And swooped and let em have it
And they had it and five dropped
Like black charabancs bursting with flames
And the other ten turned tail
Back to Deutschesland and I reported the kills
Over my radio to my girl friend
A radio WAAF called Sylvia
But then it was Bandits at 12 o'clock
So I looped the loop, strafed one, hit another
And chased a third, when suddenly, out of the sun
Came a terrible stream of chattering lead
Busting my right arm and nicking my forehead
And the blood was in my eyes
As I radioed Sylvia: Got to bale out old thing.
Adrian! Are you hurt? Nothing much. Going to jump.
Then the parachute jump down the blue lift-shaft,
Down, down – then oblivion.

And waking up in a soft-focus hospital,
And a warm pressure on my hand.
There she was, no longer a WAAF but a nurse now,
Healing my arm, telling me about the DFC
Or some gong they were insisting on
But I couldn't spend the war lying in bed
Waiting for Mr Churchill
So I sneaked out of the hospital by moonlight,
Drove my Austin 7 back to base, into my uniform,
Ready again when the loudspeaker shouted: 'Scramble'
And downing my Tizer, I ran across the tarmac...

And so did ten thousand little boys like me
In the glorious recurring Spitfire daydream.
Many years later, when I was fifty,
And my brother fifty-two, I told him my Spitfire daydream.
I used to daydream exactly the same, he said.
I asked him, what was the name of your WAAF
Who turned into a nurse?
She was called Sylvia, he said.

After Reading Hans Christian Andersen
(to my brother Jimmy, with love)

our father and mother
were kind and good
but they have left us
in this wood

As for the Fear of Going Mad

As for the fear of going mad –
It's like the fear of a teddy bear
That he may be left out in the rain
That the blackbird's beak
Will peck away his growler
That his forgotten fur will melt
Into the squelchness and the undermulch
Below greenshining skyscrapers of grass.

As for the fear of going mad –
Though night hide you away
And a blizzard blow
There are so many lanterns of love around
You'll be surely and gladly and tearfully found.

Grandfather's Footsteps

There's a guy going round so I been told
And his hands are clammy and his breath is cold
And he bothers the women and he messes up the men
Yeah Old Age hanging round again

Day after day Old Age comes creeping
Crawls on your chest while you lay sleeping
He dims your eye and he slows your pace
And scribbles his graffiti all over your face

He cuts the phone between your brain and your tongue
Kicks holes in the walls of stomach and lung
If you try to fight back he gives you the axe
With all kinds of cancer and heart attacks

He crumbles your teeth and he withers your belly
He laughs off monkey glands and Royal Jelly
He mugs the beggar and he busts the king
And he even slackens off your yo-yo string

Last night I caught Old Age in the act
Tobogganing down my digestive tract
He played my liver like a fruit machine
And used my poor heart for a trampoline

I was flying off into a terrified rage
Bubbling with insults against Old Age
Then I saw his brother Death driving into town –
Please Old Age, won't you hang around?

The Sound of Someone Walking

Why won't he stop walking
In those steady-pacing shoes
Why won't he sit and rest his feet
Listen to the news

Why won't he stop walking
With that quiet beat
Whatever the traffic I can always hear him
Moving down my street

And I think about him
Every day it seems
And I hear those footsteps
On the soundtrack of my dreams

Make him stop that walking –
At least till the day
When he walks up shakes my hand
And whispers: Time to pay.

Just a Little Bit Older

Feels like something's been happening to my skeleton
Seems like something's giving in my scaffolding
Not exactly seizing up but crackling at the corners
Spinal column fuzzing up with clusters of rust-flakes
Toe-bone joints making miniature explosions

I always thought of bones as something you could count on
Build up your framework with calcium deposits
That's what my mother sang to me but what do I do now
Now that my mother's vanished and my scaffolding is creaking
And it feels like something's been happening to my skeleton

Keep Right on to the End of the Bottle

Death is a chilly old sloucher,
His staring face as blue
As a North Pole bug.
When he shuffles, nervously,
To your bedside –
Give him a hug.

Ode to the Skull

for the glimmering eyes
two sockets
the size
of snooker-table pockets

for the nose
a sneeze of bone
to repose
itself upon

underneath
a cliff that's cleft
where perch the teeth
the few that's left

over all this
a helmet for
motor-cycling,
rain or war

you're the belfry
in which is hung
that singer of the self
the tongue

you are the scaffolding
that keeps in place
that beautiful baffled thing
the human face

without your aid
we would not know
Lew Grade
from Marilyn Monroe

and every head
would soon become
like a dead
jellyfish's bum

Skull, you're a true
protective friend
I'll stick with you
right to the end

That last quatrain?
banal and dull,
but thanks, says the brain,
to my good old skull.

My Orchard

I have a fine orchard
Where skeletons stand
In shining and
Orderly rows

And this one stands
Like a military man
And that one has
A mannequin's pose

When the night wind rises
It whistles through their sockets
With a music
Like misery

But when morning arrives
I step out of my house
And the skeletons are all
Facing me

And I choose one figure
From their bony ranks
And I pick one bone
From its frame

And I sit on the bench
And I chew that bone
And at first you know
They all taste much the same

But as I chew on
The taste of the marrow
Is always different
On my tongue

And I see the owner
Of that skeleton
When that skeleton
Was brave and young

And I smile at its beauty
And it smiles on me
Till the vision
Gradually goes

And the orchard darkens
And the skeletons stand
In shining and
Orderly rows

Poem in Portugal

Sixty years old and he's left by himself,
Strapped in the car while the shopping's done.
He watches the squat brown foreigners
Suspiciously loitering in the sun.
He sighs with relief to be missing the shops
For he can avoid the colly-wobbles
By letting the coils of his bowels settle down
Instead of bumping them over the cobbles.
He watches the tourists outsmart each other
And concludes it is much more fun
To be sixty years old and be left by himself,
Strapped in the car while the shopping's done.

Time-Bone

I chew the time-bone
Like a dog on a lawn
The school where I was buried
The grave where I was born

With my backward clockwork
Stopwatch on the go
I play on time
Every trick I know

I freak it with the hits
Of 1664
I blow it all to bits
In the Ninth World War

I set up bulgey mirrors
All around it
Mix up a thousand jig-saws
To confound it

I cut up days
With ten-minute naps
I tease time with all kinds
Of booby-traps

Now I'm sixty-two
And going on nine
I forget the present
But the future was fine

Thirty minutes later
Now I can see
Time was the dog
And the bone is me

An Ode to Dust

I know the ways of words,
Their weights and how they click together,
How they expand in summer moods, contract in winter,
The deep kind lines on the faces of some,
Others with damp and blank expressions.
Yes, I know how to talk with words
Like I know how to talk with dogs.
We get along, we can be silly together
Or weep or bop or howsyourfather...

Different with clouds.
From down here they march past with giant shoulders,
Building grandiose cathedrals,
Breaking into Turner avalanches
According to their dealings with the winds.
From a plane looking down they form cream landscapes
Gilded by the sun, silver-plated by the moon.
Slow-dancing landcapes, I often wish
William Blake could have seen them.

I can do nothing with clouds but enjoy them.
I spend more time with words and dogs,
And, though I love clouds, love them less
Than words or dogs. But more than dust.

Because dust is visible and invisible,
It bloweth where it listeth not where I list.
And dust, with no particular place to go,
Goes floating, settling, shifting, settling,
Anyoldwhere and dust consists,
Scientists tell us, of bazillions
Of flitty bits of metal, ash, cloth, grass,
Paper, wood, leather, hair and human skin
Riding the thunderstorm, surfing on the draughts.
Constellations of dust
Glitter and spin
Around the room
I'm typing in,
Falling like miniscule dry rain
Upon the floor, my desk and me.

Every word has a soul.
Every dog has a soul.
When soul rubs soul
It makes a kind of love.
But dust is the dandruff of the soul,
Dust is for philosophers –
A terrifying generalisation –
Dust is everything.

Mid-air

Once I looked out the window of a school
And saw a flying bird stop and fall dead out of the sky

Once I looked out the window of a car
And saw a flying bird stop and fall dead out of the sky

The third time I look out of a window and see this thing
Will be the moment that I die

Give Me Time – Autumn Is at the Gates
(Pushkin in a letter to M.P. Pogodin, 1st July 1828, St Petersburg)

Brown slices spread with the golden mush butter of August
And then scarlet minutes and hours from the jampot that ticks.
Time sandwiches – that's all I have time to eat.

So many words to kiss, so many sentences to massage into life,
So much verbal fondling and tumbling to be done
But the dictionary pages flicker into a blur.

Writing. Rewriting.
Mind-gliding. Day-sliding.
Cloud-drifting. Microscope-sucking.
Random sleuthing and espionage.
Searching through mountains of mud and dust.
Placing the chess-pieces on the crossword grid.
Waking with my sweaty stubble
On the bosom of my typewriter.

A child of words is born.

The child is taken to the market-place,
Held naked overhead and judged,
Acclaimed, spat at, stoned and ignored.
But by this time I'm pregnant again,
Working on the next baby.

I'd like a holiday between these exciting births,
A wordless vacation on a sea of music
So that the muscles round my eyes could relax enough
For me to gaze at the world and its people
With love but without desire
For my eyes to become as round as marbles.

Oh give me time – autumn is at the gates.

The USA is talking of a new dark age.
Iraq talks about a holy war against the forces of darkness.
Darkness screams at darkness in darkening language
About gas that nibbles up the nervous system in seconds
About bombs that swallow down whole cities.

My family, my friends, my animals,
My writing, my books, my country
And new unknown people and planets
To be gently discovered and understood.
There is so much love to be done –

Give me time – autumn is at the gates.

Slowdown

Slowdown
and simple up, flower
rid yourself
of an object an hour

Play a slow-motion
game of hopscotch
unplug the phone
and leave your watch off

Sell up your oddberries
buy less sick-a-brac
use up your woolacombes
send the hairlooms back

if it costs
leave it out in the frosts
if it's free
just leave it be

buy no kind of nothing
they advertises
borrow and lend
and bogger the prizes

spend more time in water
no time in meetings
take your son and daughter
for slowmeal eatings

get your sweatbrain done
then let down your fun
but take no advice
except from the mice

WAY OUT YONDER

Two Anti-Environmental Poems by Volcano Jones

Underarm Squirter

I hate the bloody cold I do
I hate the bloody cold
It makes me feel all blue it do
It makes me feel all old

And so I purchase aerosols
And aim them at the sky
And squirt them at the ozone layer
And here's the reason why

The more the ozone disappears
The more the sun shines through
Why? As you know, stupid, I hate the cold
I hate the bloody cold I do

Chop em Down Chop em up Burn the Lot

Don't give me trees
They throw spooky shadows on my bed
Don't give me trees
They keep nearly falling on me head
Tripping you up
With stupid great roots
Pelting you in autumn
With mushy great fruits
    Talk about rain forests
    You go in a rain forest
    You'll be lucky if you escape
    Without a fatal snakebite
    In your glove compartment
    Or your head torn off by a killer ape
Tall green buggers
Get in everyone's way
Crashed into my car
Just the other day
Don't give me trees
Give me a deadly disease
But beam me up Scottie
Don't give me fuckin trees

A Warning to Those Who Fly

If you break wind in outer space
The gas that you expel
May freeze into a solid mass
A planet made of smell

And living creatures may evolve
To praise with all their heart
The great creator of their home
The fragrant Planet Fart

Criminal Justice for Crying Out Loud – A Rant

Hello people, gather round turn up the sound and forget about
      your personal pain
Here we are stuck on an island full of traffic jams in the rain
My poetry's a rough old towel going to rub you dry again
    You'll be glowing
    And I'll be going

Now don't try slipping out the back door, zooming off down the road
They got heavies on your front and back, roadblocks every inch of
      your road
If you look like a traveller – Criminal Justice going to squash you
      like a toad

Now you heard about Criminal Justice, his honour the dreaded Judge
Cause of my disgust is Criminal Justice, that famous killing serial
      Judge
He takes mothers fathers children and he chews them up like
      Women's Institute fudge

Now you can't dodge the raindrops when the clouds decide to pour
You get soaked the rich stay dry – that's the nature of the law
Don't you know law has always been a weapon in the war between
      the rich and the poor

Long ago I heard about a goddess and Justice was her name
A famous shining naked goddess Justice was her lovely name
Now they inside outed Justice and they covered her with shame

They steal your freedom to speak
And your freedom to sing
They steal your freedom to boogie
And everything
They steal your freedom to travel
And live where you like
They steal your freedom to raise your kids
And your freedom to go on strike

Criminal Justice oh don't you dare stay out too late
Criminal Justice it's getting heavier just you wait
It's coming down like a rain of molten lead
   molten lead pouring down
    on the country and the town
      molten lead
      on your head
From the overflowing murdering mouth of the Criminal
Justice State

Full English Breakfast

Full English Breakfast
Sent from above
Butter and toast and beans
Chunky old marmalade
That's what we love
That is what England means
Full English Breakfast
Doing its best
Marching as if to war
Full English Breakfast
Standing the test
Two eggs and bacon
If I'm not mistaken
That is what England's for

Black pudding
Plum jam
Pass the cornflakes
To Pam
Grilled mushrooms
Fried bread
How's your gumboil
Uncle Fred?

Full English Breakfast
Flowing and free
Pride of the Seven Seas
Full English Breakfast
Strong English tea
Sadie likes three lumps please

Full English Breakfast
Doing its bit
Filling the English tum
England was made for Man
As God's own Frying Pan
It's the Full Monty, Mum!

Dreamcakes

   buttercream
there was buttercream
smeared in generous mounds
on top of each little sunburnt cake

   buttercream
the colour of that buttercream
was stuck somewhere
between pink and green.

   but I don't think
they can have been Earth Cakes
I never saw that particular colour
on this planet, I would remember.

the cakes themselves
were the colour of the beach
at Woolacombe in August
and they were contained
in soft corrugated semi-transparent
crumbsticky paper cups,

Some were more savoury
than others, featuring,
besides the compulsory pink-green cream
something like Heinz's Sandwich Spread
the appetiser which defied der Kaiser.

It was considered impolite
to consume an entire cake.
The etiquette: to take a bite,
about one-third, or maybe half,
then put the bitten cake back
on the communal plate
and take a bite from another one,
either bitten or unbitten.

I kept eating those cakes
happily until I woke
with a light stomach ache.

Oldverse

woman like it slow
man want it fast
man want it pronto
woman want it to last

Moving Poem

I'll call my new house 'REALITY'
Or maybe 'BOURGEOIS STATE'.
Its name will be burned on a slice of wood
And screwed to my garden gate.
When they say 'Hey, sticking a name on your house
Is a very suburban trait!'
I'll look up from the corpse I am eating
And say: 'This is the suburbs, mate.'

Stuck Together Song

I was standing in a cake shop
In this awful little town
I looked for a waitress
There was no one around
I picked myself a kind of coconut item
And a chocolate eclair but when I came to bite em
They were
Stuck Together

Well I walked out of the cakeshop
With a sack and a guitar
And a wickerwork dogbasket
And was looking for my car
I bumped into a pair of gentlemen in suits
With pinchy white faces and waterproof boots
They were
Stuck Together

Stuck together
For the rest of their life
Like the blade and handle
Of a butcher's knife
Like a handmade shoe
Made of patent leather –
Stuck Together

Me I was born on the British Isles
Like sixty million other suckers
Half of me Scottish half of me English
Half of my friends are foreign fuckers
Scotland England Northern Ireland Wales
Four different breeds of dog with droopy tails
All of us
Stuck Together

Funlovers

The floors of the oceans are dusty now
That the last of the waters have dried
With my ten thousand brothers
And ten thousand sisters
Across this crust I ride
And on twenty thousand tricycles
We'll get to the other side...

For Pam

(The song of a young woman who suddenly, unexpectedly,
breaks down. The song is close to a song which I dreamed
about an actress. She sang it in a dream I dreamed at 5 a.m.
on 7th December 1990. She had dark, shortish hair and
dark eyes in a rather blank but pretty face).

When I was born they called me Pam
Pam Pam Pam Pam Pam Pam Pam
But who is Pam? And am I Pam?
Perhaps I am, perhaps I am.

They put me outside in a pram
Pram pram pram pram pram pram pram
Am I still lying in my pram
And dreaming this? Perhaps I am.

A nasty pill in sweetest jam
Sweetest smiling scarlet jam
But am I pills? Or am I jam?
Perhaps I am, perhaps I am.

> Every word goes meaningless
> If you say it too often.
> Everybody goes meaningless
> After a time time time time time
> Pam Pam Pam Pam Pam Pam Pam

And now I do not give a damn
Damn damn damn damn damn damn damn
But am I broken, like a dam?
Perhaps I am, perhaps I am.

After the Third Election of Thatcher

O if I were Scotland I would turn my back
And climb on my horse and ride away
And if I were Wales I would turn my back
And climb on my horse and ride away

And England would stand with her purse in her hand
And her beady wee eyes filling up with dismay...

Flakes

Got any money flakes
No got none
Got any funny flakes
No got none
Got any steak flakes
No got none
Got any fake flakes
Sold the last one

Got any monkey flakes
No got none
Got any funky flakes
No got none
Got any cool flakes
No got none
Got any fool flakes
Sold the last one

I'm a resident
In a rural environment
Which is situated fifty miles
From shopping facilities for heaven's sakes
But I've come to see
This urban environment
And spend my hard-won savings on
A maximum variety of popular flakes

Got any trolley flakes
No got none
Got any brolley flakes
No got none
Got any chain flakes
No got none
Got any brain flakes
Sold the last one

Got any
None
Got any
None none
Got any
None
Got any
Buzz off son

Pull On Your Parent Hood

If your daughter becomes an actress
Buy her a typewriter
If your son becomes a writer
Buy him a jemmy
If your daughter becomes a shop assistant
Buy her a couple of chimpanzees
If your son becomes an estate agent
Chop off his hands

O Captain! My Captain! Our Fearful Trip Is Done

Your white hands tight upon the wheel,
You sold the ship off bit by bit,
Auctioned the masts, the decks, the keel
And left us sinking in the shit.

Every Monday

I was waiting my turn in the butcher's shop
Someone said: It's a shame.
Her face and her body seemed different
But her eyes were just the same.
The smile just fell right off my face,
I couldn't recall her name.

Then she said to me:

Have you heard what Joanne is up to?
She went back to that dangerous town
Trying to locate her magistrate.
Seems like he'd gone to ground.
Then luckily she met Lucy
In the burned-out shopping mall.
She brought in Flossie with her little posse
And they really had a ball.

> It was a Monday like any Monday
> Every Monday is the same
> It was a Monday like any Monday
> And I couldn't recall her name.

With a little bit of bootleg software
From the Bobby Swanberg file
They put the bite on a Trotskyite
So he hipped them for a while.
Round the clock they watched the Galaxy Hotel
From a rented motorboat.
It was ten to one on that the fox had gone
But they had to play every note.

> It was a Monday like any Monday
> Every Monday is the same
> It was a Monday like any Monday
> And I couldn't recall her name.

Well human beings are human beings,
You know everybody has to blink
And the Monktown pack crawled around the back
And soon the water turned pink.
Well Joanne she rang me later
From the special callbox at the Zoo.
She was cut off, sure, but just before –
She told me that she must see you...

It was a Monday like any Monday
If you play the Monday game
It was a Monday like any Monday
And I couldn't recall her name.

Screw It Yourself
(the first and last in a series of DIY poems)

With each turn it do make within its Hole
A Screw should advance towards its Goal.
If it fails in this Task, let the Blame fall
On the Screw, the Screw-Driver or the Wall.

Seasonal Fanfare

It sounded like a squashed ostrich
And it smelled like a Pharaoh's tomb
And it spread like a rumour at the BBC
Throughout the festive room.
Oh the young were convulsed with guffawing
And the old folded up with gloom –
It was the First Fart of Christmas
And it echoed like the Cracker of Doom.

The Sons of Fred

*(after misreading a line in a Peter Porter poem referring
to 'the sons of Freud' as 'the sons of Fred')*

The Sons of Fred are on the go
On the boil on the fiddle on the hop
The Sons of Fred want you to know
That Fredlessness is definitely going to stop

The Sons of Fred are on the booze
With a song for the living and the dead
The Sons of Fred shout out the news
That everyone will soon be a Son of Fred

Oh yes!
Get that!
Put on your blue galoshes
And your Freddian hat.
If you meet a son of Freda
Nick a fiver off the bleeder.
If you meet a son of Freud
Splash that dusty humanoid.
But if you meet a son of Fred
Just repeat what I have said:

The Sons of Fred are on the go...

Icarus Talking to His Dad

since I first dreadfully fitted my fingers
into the tipless gloves under the angle of the wings
and you criss-crossed my body with the straps
which would draw me close under and into the wings
and closer till they reacted with my shoulder blades
as if they had grown there

you always told me babies are born with wings
but on the seventh day a visitor comes
and clips them off and anoints the stubs
with anti-feather growing ointment
only the wing stubs the shoulder blades still sometimes
dream about flying
and on this dream we will build our freedom

it is about freedom, you said, you insisted,
remember always flying is about freedom
it is about wheeling and tumbling and falling through clouds
it is about laughing and exploring the possibilities of the body
it is about playing tag with swallows
and the attempt to become as free as air

it is not about conquest or achievement or record-breaking
it is not just for you
it is freedom and it is for everyone
that is why I have worked day and night
and when I became blind worked on blindly
because my intelligent fingers longed
to complete the great task –
the first pair of working human wings

just the first pair, I've made them so that
if they work,
any fool can make a thousand pairs

they had to be simple
there had to be a simple way, a best way
and there was and I found it
as a village finds a path down through rocks to the sea

and you also said, not too near the sun, son,
that was your joke, always with a blind man's wink –
not too near the sun, son

November/December 1989 in Romania

*(to a Romanian teacher of English who spoke about
that time to a conference in Vienna three months later)*

She stood there like a sigh.

She said: 'I was so hopeless.
I felt I would burst.
I didn't burst.
Then, in that moment, everything burst.'

She laughed,
Her laughter broken up by sigh after sigh.

If You're Lookin' for Trouble
You've Come to the Wrong Place

(for the CND Rally, Trafalgar Square, 1994)

This is a rally in the cause of Peace.
You'd rather have Conflict? Then I suggest
You join the Army or the Police –
(If you can pass the intelligence test).

FOR LOVE
AND FRIENDSHIP

My Father's Land

1

Sand-dunes
And sand-dunes
And St Andrews

A blueboard sky
Scribbled all over with seagulls
Who spell out chemical formulae

Sand-dunes
And sand-dunes
And St Andrews students

Scarlet-gowned
Against the grey and glittering town
Jock Mitchell, the young scientist

Sand-dunes
And sand-dunes
And the bottle dungeon in St Andrews

There was a bottle dungeon
Let into the ground
They lowered its one prisoner
Down the neck
Into the depths of the bottle

Down in the bottle
The darkness was total
Waves smashed against the walls outside
First the prisoner went mad,
Said the guide, later he went blind

Sand-dunes
And sand-dunes
And the North Sea
And France

2

1914-1918
He descended into Hell
Which is a labyrinth of trenches
Slashed out of chilling, killing mud.
All his old friends died there
And he crouched with his new comrades –
Obscene diseases, shells and rats,
Madness and blindness.
Down in the bottle
The darkness was total –
Sent, by the King,
To Hell in a kilt –
My gentle young father.

3

Sand-dunes
And sand-dunes
And Woolacombe

And on the farthest wave-slapped rock
Towards the end of Baggy Point
Alone in a salty zone of his own
Face brown as his shoes
Body white as his teeth
Fishing all day and catching nothing,
And happy that nothing was to be caught –
My father.

4

My mother's laughter
And the laughter of her friends
Tumbling out of the french windows and beyond them

I'm on the patio paving stones
Exterminating a city of Ants
I am Bomber Command
With a seething kettle.

And beyond me
The warm-swarming lawn is sloping
Under the weight of three apple trees,
Their ancient trunks bulging,
Leaning to one side,
Each bearing a deadly, sticky circle.

Beside that lawn
My bright-haired brother's head
Level with the cabbages
As he excavates
A system of trenches
Which he will fit with a sliding roof
And electric light and a drainage pump,
Putting my primitive
Hole in the ground for hiding in
To simple, muddy shame.

And way beyond and behind all this,
Past the experimental asparagus,
Hidden from family, friends and Germans,
In his bamboo city streets of raspberry canes
Stands my middle-aged father, Jock.

He is five foot six.
You look at his strong brown eyes and say:
He must have laughed a lot.
You look at his strong brown eyes and say:
He must have lost a lot.

He squashes up his mouth
As he kicks the blade of his spade
Down into the rich earth of Surrey.
When he rests
He reaches into his salty old sports jacket,
Into the pocket he keeps full of bread-crumbs
And rewards the robin who follows him everywhere,
Like a small boy with sticky-up hair.

And he is still there, in the raspberry canes,
And soon my mother will bring him his tea
So he doesn't have to come into the house
And be polite to her friends.

A Late Elegy for Jock Mitchell

The Imperial Tobacco Company
Tore my father from his family
After much terror and agony.

Four years in the trenches could not break
His body. He died for the sake
Of sucking Players and Gold Flake.

He looked like an old child that day.
'We love you,' was all that I could say.
He said: 'It's awful,' then turned away.

Goodnight, Stevie

Over an ocean of silvery froth,
Past mammoths in forests of moonlit myth
Flies a zig-zagging, incandescent moth –
The poetry of Stevie Smith.

With Love to Alan and Shelagh Hancox

*'I lost the sight in one eye this week & after deep tests am on
a massive dose/course of steroids in an attempt to save the
other...Ah well, I still have one & my still alive mind's eye.'
– Alan Hancox in a letter to me, 9th November 1990. For this
poem I have borrowed several of his warm phrases from letters.
Alan, the friend of many writers, kept a bookshop and ran
the Cheltenham Literature Festival.*

A feast for the mind's eye –
A wilful waterfall of paperbacks,
Then walking through the sub-aquatic lighting
Along that underground river of carpet,

Through a magical arch to the wizard's cave
Made of the best books in the world,
Their spines glow blue, gold, green and red –
Much water has flowed etcetera –
Alan, I love to see your friendly name.

A feast for everyone –
Friendships new and friendships old
Consolidated and renewed
And something, something in the air –
Ted Hughes builds limestone walls of words,
Angela Carter rides the tightrope elephant –
The literary life-force raking up
The multi-coloured leaves into a bonfire –
Something THEY said couldn't be done.
Alan, your friendship was a festival.
You wanted your last to be your best
And so – your mind's eye winks at me – it was.
You loved your books well, your friends even better.
Alan, I love to see your friendly name.

Reggie Smith in Paradise
(for Di with love)

In the slums of the Golden City
With a badge saying: Devils Want Peace!
He wallops the words in a public bar
With Dylan and Louis MacNeice.
God's Broadcasting Company sacked him
For cheeking the Holy Ghost
By calling it: 'You spooky Tory',
But the zillionfold Heavenly Host
Have all bought Olivia's latest.
Jerry refills each glass
While Reggie's explaining to Shakespeare
That Heaven is based upon class...

For Michael Gough on His Birthday

Like a favourite tree
By a grassy track
Which children pat
And it brings them good luck

Like a limestone stream
Speaking over and over
Its shining poems –
Green, glass and silver

Like a peace-filled well
Like a waterbird display
Like our dear friend Mick Gough –
Happy Birthday!

Brightness of Brightness
(for Trix Craig on her seventeenth birthday, 3rd July 1992)

Brightness of an estuary –
Glittering seabirds in spirals of light
Over the molten bars of golden mud.
Brightness of a forest glade –
A sun-pool waiting the arrival
Of a shy, gliding family of deer.
Brightness of a midnight river
Playing like Jack B. Yeats
With the harlequin lights of the city.
Brightness of a black and white dog
Bouncing above and below the bracken.

Brightness of those eyes
Brightness of that hair

Brightness of memory
Brightness of the good times
Brightness of that palace in Carlton Hill
With its tumbling tower and fantasy plumbing
Where all the troubles of the world
Dissolved in Irish laughter.

Brightness of the house in Snape
With furious Scrabble by a furious fire
And Christmas feasts the whole year round
With butterlight and creamlight,
Meringue-light and dreamlight
And the light of blue bubble fountains
In a deep goblet of gin and tonic.
O brightness of gravy, brightness of wine,
Brightness of Trix's voice
And the best company in the world.

For her eyes look on the no-good human race
With endless forgiveness, endless affection,
And her heart dances around
Catherine of the deep wild eyes
Michael of the laughing waterfall
Fergus the fine young tree
Blanche the new whirling little moon
And her two shadows
Those finest of dogs
Meggie and Tashy
And uncountable friends
Some alive here and loving her
Some gone but still alive in her heart
In the brightness of that heart
As all-embracing as the sunlight
Brightness of brightness
Light of a thousand lives
Brightness of brightness
Beloved Trix.

For My Old Friend Jeremy Brooks

April sun kissing the blossoms awake
April air tickling the waterside grassleaves
And, growing out of that grass
An honest wooden chair.

The good old chair supports you –
Your face in the sunfall,
The sun along the river.
Eleanor leans to listen to your voice.

April: rocks in the river –
Some bowling and skidding along
In underwater fits and starts,
Others looming up into the air
As castles, dopey monsters, mosshaired giants –

And I admire them all,
Wondering as I walk the turf
Which rock's your own, your favourite,
The secret island of your great heart.

April in the valley of beauty.
The somersaulting, holiday-shouting waters
Celebrate their fizzing, bumping journey
Towards the fabulous sea.

Your face in the sun surrounded by friends –
The cottage of many caves,
The simple complicated trees
And the best grass in the world.

And, all around your life,
Love, like the singing of soaring words.
Love, like the poems of a thousand birds.

Maybe Maytime

(for Celia)

There was a moment in a garden.
There was a moment in a garden –
Small green spiders trapezing down through
Yellow spotlights in that great green tent.
Something was singing with the voice of apples.
A breeze touched my cheekbone, or perhaps it was a fingertip.

There was a moment, there was a sandpath,
Pine-cone-scattered and swerving its way
Among the red-bark trees with their polished roots.
There was a snub-nosed rowing boat
Stuck forever among hissing rushes –
On the water's surface, a famous insect city.

There was a moment, there was a voice,
Wild as your hair and gentle as your breasts.
And a raucous old train rattled its way around
 the rim of the valley.

I might have been five, perhaps fifty-five,
Could have been October, maybe Maytime,
But I know it was you, my love,
I know it was you
Because look, here's the mark, right over my heart.

Celia's Flower

Nineteen Dollars Ninety-Five Cents Haiku

Brand-new pyjamas:
At dawn I find the price-tag
Stuck on me pongo.

Sometimes Awake

deep in the centre of her breasts
two nameless flowers grow
their small leaves furled
their petals curling
with porcelain blueness
like the morning skies
on the fifth of april

sometimes awake
and sometimes asleep
and sometimes both at once
I've gazed so often on those two blue flowers
to see them gazing back at me
with all the love I ever thirsted for

For Me and You

Throat is such a beautiful word
Throats were often
Sliced by the sword
The thrush sings
With an angel's throat
As we sail past the stars
In an orange-skin boat

Exit

Out of the battered backdoor of the ark in Arkansas
Out of the songs of swamp-bewildered birds
Out of a cradle on the moon
Stumble the radiant, hilarious herds
Of moose with antlers all askew
All of them well nonplussed with love for you

Thank You for All the Years We've Had,
Thank You for All the Years to Come

My blue hand stretched out of sight in the blizzard's white
For one rose among the snows of Everest
And my chest and mouth ached for the touching of your breast
For I loved to be loved by your love more than anyone knows

In Sweetmeat Street I lay in the guttering muck
The crowd laughed aloud at me the Semi-Human Dungheap
But you jumped from the hump of your camel, lifted me up
And saved me, sunned me and lay me beside you to sleep

I was scared by the stare of the white-masked moon
For I knew those two cold Os were the cratery eyes of Death
But pink morning dawned as you rose over me
And I cried golden molten tears of happiness...

The Lake Is a Piano
(for Jude on her birthday)

the lake is a piano

as the sky whispers midnight
the odd-faced Moon walks in
in his white tie and tails
he sits down on the grassbound bank
removes his silver gloves and plays
with gentle ripples and a few pretty splashes
a silver sonata
for Jude with love

the lake is a piano

goats steaming in the dawn
the chickens flowering into light
and a sweet white scattering of doves
as that old show-off Sun
smiles his way across
the green slopes of the stage
and his hot fingers
set the water boiling into waterspouts
and the wild fountain of
a golden concerto
for Jude with love

the lake is a piano

Evening enters in her evening dress
with starry ear-rings and a sighing breeze
and because the world's so beautiful
she plays the blues
because the world's so sad she makes it funny
and Evening sings a song that says
that love is all that ever mattered
and we all love you Jude
all night all day all evening
our love for you is like a lake
and you have all our love

An Open Window

Love is an open window and the breeze
Breathing into the bedroom from that window

And love is the towering, tearful tree
Seen in the frame of an open window

And love is the hot-blooded sky beyond
Longing to tear its clouds off for the sun

And love is how we lie here, looking and longing,
Under the gaze of an open window.

    C'an Torrent, Deya.

Doreen Webster Teaches Us a Zulu Dance

You watch and listen
And if you don't watch and listen
You are lost for good

Ode to Deborah Levy

Deborah
Reminds me of a zeborah
Except that she's a biped
And not striped.

Your Name

(for Sasha, 7th November 1994)

an orangey name
a flamey name
a flashing silkenscarf of a name

a foresty name
a sunmisted name
a climbing-frame in a library name

a righteous rocking name that dares to stomp
   on the lugubrious floor of 1994
      the dance of the love of life
         love of life
         love of life

a name that smiles
   singing as it flies
a name that thrills the heart
   of father mother
      sister lover
and all the animals

   Sasha
the name you wear
illuminate and warm and magic

   Sasha
whose secret meaning is
love and be loved

      beloved
      Sasha

Happy Breakfast, Hannah, on Your Eighteenth Birthday

Today you sit down to a proper breakfast.
Yesterday you were seventeen
On the Sunny Side of the Century
Arranged for ukulele and spotty pyjamas.

The day before yesterday you were twelve
All woolly hat, armsful of homework,
The largest eyes in the known world
And sudden laughter beside a lake.

The day before that you were six and a bit
In enormous boots and a housewife hat
Chasing the vicar with your deadly gamp.

And the day before that, eighteen years ago,
The midwife said:
'This one's been here before'
As you came up really bright into the light.

And I wish you a house in a wood
Within the sighing of the sea
Animals around your feet
And the music of peacetime to dance your own dance
And all the love in the world, lovely Hannah,
As you come up bright into the light.

For Amy

Poetry can be a lonely walk
Down a dark forest pathway
Without an end.
So it lifts the heart to see the brightness
Of a welcoming new friend.

What's that wonderful, warmful light
Shining out a thousand miles?
All the animals of the world start dancing –
When Amy smiles.

Sam's Way

You take your overcoat.
You lay it on the ground, back downwards, front open,
Sleeves outstretched to the side and up.
You stand at the top of the coat, feet just above the neck.
You bend down and stick your arms down the sleeves.
You stand up, pulling the coat over your head.
You find you are standing in your overcoat
And everybody is astonished.

A Flying Song

(for Caitlin Georgia Isabel Stubbs, born 18th April 1993)

Last night I saw the sword Excalibur
It flew above the cloudy palaces
And as it passed I clearly read the words
Which were engraven on its blade
    And one side of the sword said Take Me
    The other side said Cast Me Away

I met my lover in a field of thorns
We walked together in the April air
And when we lay down by the waterside
My lover whispered in my ear
    The first thing that she said was Take Me
    The last thing that she said was Cast Me Away

I saw a vision of my mother and father
They were sitting smiling under summer trees
They offered me the gift of life
I took this present very carefully
    And one side of my life said Take Me
    The other side said Cast Me Away

Reaching for the Light

Crocus in flames
Never burns up
Dew comes dropping
And it fills the cup
Darkness falls
Petals close up for the night
But when the dawn paints them
They start
Reaching for the light

Baby swimming
Inside your womb
Searching for brightness
In that warm gloom
Well blood is red
And milk is white
Out dives the baby
And she's
Reaching for the light

    Light springs the life in everyone
    That's why the planets dance around the sun
    Light makes the heart and the spirit rise
    That's why Caitlin tries to touch your eyes

See the appletree
Standing there
Stretching blossoms
In the shining air
See Caitlin growing
With all her sweet might
I want the moon
Mum
I'm reaching for the light

To Caitlin Riding on My Shoulders

When you're up there
High in the air
Riding upon my shoulder
You play with my hair
Like it's some kind of rare
White grass growing
On an old pink boulder
Don't you know I'm underneath
With my detachable teeth
Thinking how wonderfully wild you are
So hang on tight
Pull my scalp off that's all right
Your ever-loving Grandpapa

Stufferation

Lovers lie around in it
Broken glass is found in it
Grass
I like that stuff

Tuna fish get trapped in it
Legs come wrapped in it
Nylon
I like that stuff

Eskimos and tramps chew it
Madame Tussaud gave status to it
Wax
I like that stuff

Elephants get sprayed with it
Scotch is made with it
Water
I like that stuff

Clergy are dumbfounded by it
Bones are surrounded by it
Flesh
I like that stuff

Harps are strung with it
Mattresses are sprung with it
Wire
I like that stuff

Carpenters make cots of it
Undertakers use lots of it
Wood
I like that stuff

Dirty cigarettes are lit by it
Pensioners get happy when they sit by it
Fire
I like that stuff

Johnny Dankworth's alto is made of it, most of it *
Scoobdidoo is composed of it †
Plastic
I like that stuff

Elvis kept it in his left-hand pocket
Little Richard made it zoom like a rocket
Rock 'n' Roll
Ooh my soul
I like that stuff

Apemen take it to make them hairier
I ate a ton of it in Bulgaria
Yoghurt
I like that stuff

Man-made fibres and raw materials
Old rolled gold and breakfast cereals
Platinum linoleum
I like that stuff

Skin on my hands
Hair on my head
Toenails on my feet
And linen on the bed

Well I like that stuff
Yes I like that stuff
The earth
Is made of earth
And I like that stuff

* Jazz musician John Dankworth used to play a plastic saxophone.

† Scoobdidoo was a fistful of kind of multi-coloured pieces of plastic which
were a playground craze in the 1950s. It was a sad sort of toy, nothing like
the exciting Hula Hoop of the same period.

Silence

I held silence
Like a globe
I held silence
And it glowed

BOTY

Boty Goodwin

(*obituary from* The Guardian)

The last time we saw Boty Goodwin, our extra daughter, she was happy, blonde, optimistic and planning her thirtieth birthday party. That was about four weeks ago, in Boston, Massachusetts. Boty had flown in from LA for 24 hours to see Adrian's new show *Tyger Two* and to spend a little time with us, the parents she'd adopted. Then she flew back to the California Institute of the Arts to give her final show before a board of examiners.

This was a presentation on November 6th of stories she'd written about her life performed against a background of beautiful wallpaper which illustrated key images from her history. At 29, she was already a brilliant artist/writer/performer – and her show delighted her examiners, who congratulated her, offered her a scholarship and encouraged her to take her Master's Degree in both writing and fine art.

On November 9th she repeated the show for her fellow-students, who were dazzled and exhilarated. All her life Boty celebrated whatever was worth celebrating. That night she partied with her friends. At some point she was given a drug which killed her. She died in her studio in the early hours of November 10th of an accidental overdose of heroin.

Boty wasn't a junkie or a suicide. Nor was she a martyr or a role model. She was a lovely, funny, very talented young woman who made one stupid, fatal mistake.

Boty Goodwin was an orphan. Her mother was Pauline Boty – one of England's finest pop painters, an actress whose beauty was admired by everyone and whose shining intelligence enlightened her friends. Pauline was the painter of *The Only Blonde in the World* – perhaps the greatest and most lively painting of Marilyn Monroe.

Pauline met and fell in love with Clive Goodwin. He was a working-class actor, handsome, witty and hip, who became editor of the influential magazine *Encore* and later worked on the TV arts programme *Tempo* as right-hand man to Kenneth Tynan.

Pauline and Clive married. But shortly after she became pregnant, Pauline was diagnosed as suffering from a rare form of leukaemia. She gave birth to a daughter and died shortly afterwards. Clive decided that the baby should be named Boty. Boty spent her first years living with her loving grandparents in Surrey. Clive was nervous about looking after a little girl by himself, but we encouraged him to bring Boty to live with him in his large South Kensington flat.

The first time he looked after her on his own, Clive was terrified, so they both came to stay with us in the beautiful Yorkshire farmhouse where we lived at the time. Boty and our two daughters, Sasha and Beattie, who were around her age, became very attached to each other. It was during one of these visits that Clive told us: 'If anything should ever happen to me, you will have Boty to live with you, won't you?' We laughed, of course, our friends didn't die in those days. We laughed, but we agreed.

In 1968 Clive founded the *Black Dwarf*, that fine raging left-wing magazine in which, for a short time, socialists, artists, pacifists, anarchists, poets and communists formed a volatile alliance. By now Clive was also literary agent for most of the best left-wing playwrights in Britain.

One day, when Boty was nearly 12, Clive flew to Los Angeles to negotiate with Warren Beatty and Trevor Griffiths about the movie *Reds*. They met in the Beverly Wiltshire Hotel. During the meeting Clive drank one glass of wine. But he was suddenly attacked by a headache and had to leave. In the lobby of the hotel he staggered and vomited.

The hotel staff, thinking he was drunk, called the Los Angeles police. Clive was handcuffed and thrown into a police cell, where he died, alone, of a cerebral haemorrhage.

There was a big memorial meeting in a London theatre – with songs and speeches and poems. Boty, nearly 12 years old, not only came to the meeting, but insisting on appearing in a sketch of her own devising, in which she and Clive's secretary were trying to contact Clive by phone. Everyone knew right away that Boty, somehow, would survive.

Until she was 16, Boty lived with her grandparents and came to us in London for weekends and holidays. But she had lived with Clive in the centre of radical, bohemian, rocking London and she longed to return.

When she was 16 she chose to live with us and go to the local comprehensive. By now she was one of the family, a maker of laughter, a setter of style and a wonderful peacemaker in a sometimes stormy family. Our proudest moment came when Boty signed a card to us – lots of love from your extra daughter.

Four years after her father's death the Los Angeles Police and the Beverly Wilshire finally settled out of court and Boty had financial independence. Her beauty and intelligence and wit attracted hundreds of friends and admirers. But she worried that some people were after her money – and a few of them were.

Boty believed fiercely in education. She knew that education for women is the only real way to freedom, but she also knew and understood politically the huge advantage she had over most other women because of her money. She was able to choose for herself to study at the California Institute of the Arts and pay her own way. But money didn't corrupt her. She remained true to her Clive and Pauline's principles while developing her own political philosophy.

Her family and friends and teachers and fellow-students are devastated. Maybe this will silence a few of those voices which whisper that 'smack is cool if you know how to handle it' and play on the glamour of dead and alive junkie rock stars to make heroin a fashionable poison. We feel both empty and angry about Boty's death. But we and her extra sisters who loved her so utterly are immensely proud of her talented, shining life.

ADRIAN & CELIA MITCHELL

Boty Goodwin was born on 12th February 1966.
She died on 10th November 1995.

154

The Forest and the Lake

*(for Clive Goodwin, Pauline Boty and their daughter
Boty Goodwin, written soon after Clive's death).*

the forest laughed

plenty to laugh at –
squirrels at their gymnastics,
motorways full of fanatical ants
carrying out their looney missions,
overdressed pheasants holding fashion parades
watched by the rabbiting rabbits –

the forest laughed a lot

sun-washed clearings,
small thickets dark with grief –
it was a good forest to go to,
swaying and sheltering,
welcoming as a woolly, brown-eyed dog

one day the forest turned its head
and realised it grew beside a lake

the lake was liquid light

there were deeps with wisdom fish
long as your leg,
there were shallows with quick fish
tinier than pins,
swallows skimming and surfing,
a plump of ducks at their pleasure-boating

the lake looked down at the fish and smiled
the lake looked up at the waterbirds and smiled

the lake looked at the forest and smiled

and from that day
it was lake and forest
forest and lake

so lovely so lively
shining and shadow
the laughing forest
and the shining lake
green hand holding blue hand
a landscape of glory
in which so many of us wandered happily...

only the bird of badness sang: not long

and the earth shook twice
and the lake shook dark
and the forest shook still

dawn finds us watching
as a green and blue striped boat
drifts over smoking waters
up to the shaded shore

and, nearly twelve years old,
half forest and half lake,
out of the boat steps Boty

The Boty Sign

*(while Boty was studying in California it was part of my
happy duty to write verse for her birthdays – this was the last
one, based on the idea of the Hollywood Sign being replaced)*

England with its sticky shadows
beloved puddles of despair
where colonels wallow and milk-maids drown
or are ground underground
by devil-yellow tarmac machines
shovelling their tons of darkness
along the miserly streets
built of one billion bricks

You light it up
like a buzzing bright sign in the sky
You light it up
like the forty-fourth of July
You light it up
like only a blonde can shine
And we're happy to dance under
THE BOTY SIGN

Some keep their soul
like a dandruff budgie in a cage
They die of television tremors
They die of extreme young age
You let your soul fly
through eagle and tornado rage
You let your soul fly
it flies so fine
It does aerobatics illuminated by
THE BOTY SIGN

Around the wild world
the skies are flashing sweeter than sex
Boggled people looking up
and cricking their collarbound necks
Is it a bluewhite comet?
What's those rays coming from it?
Is it a turbo-hummingbird? A superfizz wine?
Nope ya dope – it's
THE BOTY SIGN
It's the farfunny, flamehoney, burnbutter, flameflutter – Fine fine
fine – it's THE BOTY SIGN!

A Flower for Boty

Eloquent art
Speaking straight to the heart
Fills the critic with numbing dismay
For eloquent art
Speaking straight to the heart
Leaves the critic with fuck-all to say

157

Good Luck Message to Boty with Flowers
Before Her Finals at Cal Arts

With the Style of the Beatles
The Flash of Jean Harlowe
And the Funkiness of Frida Kahlo
Plus the Fire of Blake
And the Wings of Shelley
C'mon Boty
Give it plenty of Welly

Telephone

Telephone told me that you were dead
Now I hate every telephone's stupid head
I'd rather sit here turning to a block of stone
Than pick up any snake of a telephone

Every Day

Every day we're going to talk to you Boty
Tell you the ridiculous News
The Politics of Bebopalula for All
And the Meaning of Red Suede Shoes

Every day we'll have Visions of you Boty
Dressed up like a Birthday Cake
Every day we're going to listen to your Voice
And your Laughter like a Trumpet Break

Every day we're going to see you clearer
Stomping on a faraway Starry Floor
Every day we'll edge a little bit nearer
Till we Dance with our Boty once more

(I wrote that last poem with a beautiful new fountain pen. I saw it at London Airport on my way to fly to Los Angeles for Boty's Memorial Meeting. The pen was flecked in various shades of silvery blue and I couldn't afford it. But I heard Boty whisper to me – Go on – buy it! Get blue ink and only use it to write poems. And when I paid for it, I heard Boty laughing.)

For Boty

Down on this planet
where we waver and wander
lost among the towering hours

Down on this planet
when an apple tree dies
there is a long leaning
and a slow falling through the years
until the moss-kissed insect-lively trunk
rests in its bed of grass
and becomes part of the grass

And down on this planet
if you drop a ball on the pavement
its bounces become smaller
till it finds a resting curb or gutter

Things fall and take their time in falling
and then they take their rest

But I don't see you as falling darling
you seem to move
among our lives
like waves of the sea
like a mist of tears sun-touched with laughter
like a slow snowfall
like bonfire smoke
and the swirl of scarlet leaves

Especially When It Snows

(for Boty)

especially when it snows
and every tree
has its dark arms and widespread hands
full of that shining angelfood

especially when it snows
and every footprint
makes a dark lake
among the frozen grass

especially when it snows darling
and tough little robins
beg for crumbs
at golden-spangled windows

ever since we said goodbye to you
in that memorial garden
where nothing grew
except the beautiful blank-eyed snow

and little Caitlin crouched to wave goodbye to you
down in the shadows

especially when it snows
and keeps on snowing

especially when it snows
and down the purple pathways of the sky
the planet staggers like King Lear
with his dead darling in his arms

especially when it snows
and keeps on snowing